APOSTASIA

A CORRUPT CHURCH FOR A CORRUPT AGE

Danny McDowell

Printed in the United States of America.

ISBN: 978-1-4269-5912-7 (sc)
ISBN: 978-1-4269-5911-0 (e)

Trafford rev. 03/14/2011

 www.trafford.com

North America & international
toll-free: 1 888 232 4444 (USA & Canada)
phone: 250 383 6864 ♦ fax: 812 355 4082

All profit realized from the sale of this book will go to our Non Profit, Non Governmental Organization in Uganda East Africa for the express purpose of helping the poorest of the poor. We are the New Testament Fellowship of Entebbe Uganda.

Ps-94:16
16 Who will rise up for me against the wicked?
Who will take a stand for me against evildoers?

ACKNOWLEDGEMENTS

There are actually three individuals that have influenced me most in my understanding of Church Eschatology, which is the bulk of the teaching in this book. From those who convinced me most, I have moved on to research and discover as many errant doctrines as I can. This book reflects only a few of those errant and abhorrent doctrines and traditions that I have discovered over the past thirteen years of study. It is these three men that got me started on this journey and I am eternally grateful.

Marvin Rosenthal---The pre-wrath rapture of the Church

I was searching the shelves of a Christian book store in 1998, looking for something "new" in Bible Prophecy. I had read all the pre-trib books I could get my hands on because I was a staunch pre-tribulationist even though I had serious questions about my own doctrine. I sat down in that store and began to read Rosenthal's book. I sat there for about two hours. I could not believe how easily things fell into place, and how the book of Revelation began to open up to me in an understandable way. "Continuity" was the best word to describe that work. I do not KNOW Marvin Rosenthal personally, but I am grateful for his influence in my life.

Gene Bacon----Rapture----Truth or Consequences

Another man who I have never met. I picked up Gene's radio broadcast soon after being convinced by Rosenthal's explanation of the "rapture and tribulation." Scripture upon scripture, line upon line, precept upon precept, to the point that I was obsessed with spreading the "truth about the rapture". Because such a doctrine [post-tribulationism] was so severely shunned in evangelical circles [especially in the Bible Belt] where I live, I had no avenue in which to release the information that persistently flooded my mind. I turned to RADIO as an outlet. I taught doctrine and eschatology for two years on Radio station W.H.O. AM in Stuart Virginia. I taught the same at an Independent Baptist Church in Winston Salem, North Carolina which led to a Cable television series on "The Seventy Weeks of Daniel". That program aired several times per week for twelve consecutive weeks. Gene Bacon is responsible for a GREAT VALIDATION of what Rosenthal had led me into.

Dave MacPherson-----Famous rapture Watchers. The Rapture plot.

Dave MacPherson absolutely SEALED the package with "Famous Rapture Watchers", a paper showing the doctrinal position of the Church [regarding the "tribulation of the Saints"] from the First Century to Contemporary theologians." His many books follow the origin and development of Pre-Tribulationism from the early 1800's till now. He thoroughly crushes false doctrine and exposes those who teach it. Pre-Tribulationists fear him because they fear being exposed. It is because of his writing that I am convinced that I can face ANYONE in the world in debate on this issue. I was once involved in an e-mail debate with a renowned Pre-tribulationist. When he discovered that I was utilizing material written by Dave MacPherson he [Thomas] disappeared like "Ice in Death Valley." In my opinion, Dave MacPherson is the greatest Post Trib apologist in the world today. You cannot do justice to your studies in Bible Eschatology without reading Dave MacPherson.

None of the three of these men have influenced my writing beyond the study of Bible Eschatology, I do not know their opinions on other matters discussed in this book.

in memory of

Dorothy Sylvia Bolton
and
------all the elderly women [Jaja] of East Africa who have
sacrificed their latter years to raise and care for the
HIV orphans in their towns and villages.

TABLE OF CONTENTS

INTRODUCTION

Modern day evangelicals have succumbed to many late, and historic, erroneous doctrines, practices and heresies. The purpose of this book is to take a close look at a few of these errors strictly through the clear lens of the Old and New Testaments. I will also present positions long held by the greatest theologians and doctrinal apologists of the Church age, reaching all the way back to the Apostles themselves. The question that I present is this---"how reliable is a faith that fluctuates with the passing of time"? How can one place his trust in something that is constantly in motion? The New Testament speaks of our faith being founded in terms such as "foundation, cornerstone, a sure hope", and many other examples that cause us to know in a very certain way that Our God is real and never changes. His Apostles reveal the certainty of God's word and plan for his Church. The Bible was never intended to be a spiritual SLOT MACHINE by which we simply PULL THE HANDLE and receive into our hearts, that which presents itself by chance. The Bible is our sure foundation revealing the past, present, and future of the Church. It is not simply a Bingo Parlor in which we hold our breath while the latest popular preacher comes up with the winning numbers. Our God is a ROCK. He is immovable. He does not change his mind in the passing of time. Some of the doctrines that we will look at will be shocking to some and ignorantly defended by others. "Doctrine" separates the sheep from the goats, the wheat from the tares, the dross from that which is pure and tried by fire. This is my attempt to bring attention to this critical issue.

CHAPTER I

The Rapture Question

The rapture of the Church is a topic that is often discussed and preached in the Church today. The fact is, the word Rapture is nowhere to be found in the Bible. The only reference to the receiving of God's people unto Christ is called "the gathering." Because the term "rapture" is so commonly used in the Church, I will use that term for the sake of clarity. And now, a synopsis of the most popular scenario regarding the "rapture"---- the gathering of God's elect.

-------------------------------- *Pre-Tribulation Synopsis*

Regarding the gathering of God's elect to meet Christ in the air, "Pre-tribulationism" is the most popular doctrine in the evangelical Church today. It is a Church heresy which is found in no teachings or expositions by theologians of the Church prior to 1830. Hear me clearly----there is not one single written exposition supporting pre-tribulation theology pre-dating the year 1830. If you believe this statement to be untrue, then you have a formidable challenge ahead of you. A synopsis of pre-tribulationism follows.

1. The rapture is an imminent event. It could take place at any moment---it has been imminent since the Day of Pentecost in the book of Acts. All born again believers will be taken in the pre-trib rapture. All the children of the world [under the age of accountability] will be taken in the rapture as well.

2. Soon after the rapture, antichrist will rise to power and establish a seven year peace agreement between Israel and her Arab neighbors.

3. The signing of a seven year peace covenant will trigger seven years of tribulation.

4. All of earth's people who did not know Christ will be "left behind" to suffer the terrors of seven years of tribulation---the wrath of almighty God.

5. 3 1/2 years into the tribulation, antichrist will abominate a newly rebuilt Jewish Temple in Jerusalem.

6. The second half of the tribulation [great tribulation] will begin---horrors on earth.

7. The Church will be in heaven [for the seven years of tribulation] receiving their rewards and in the marriage supper of the lamb while earth's inhabitants are suffering the horrors of the tribulation.

8. At the end of the seven years, Christ will return in clouds of glory with his saints and destroy the wicked, antichrist, and false prophet, and cast Satan into a fiery place to be restrained for 1000 years.

9. The millennial reign of Christ will begin.

We will begin with the Doctrine of Imminence. Proponents of this doctrine emphatically declare that the gathering of the Church, to meet Christ in the air, is an imminent event. The very word "imminent" [in dictionary terms] means "at any time, without preceding signs or indicators, any moment now." In other words, Christ could return at any moment to gather his Church into the air. This position is based on their understanding of I Thess 4:16 and other erroneously interpreted verses. Many also declare that the "rapture" has been imminent throughout the Church age, beginning on the Day of Pentecost when the Church was born. Some have moved the goal-post beyond the penning of the book of Revelation because of the obvious challenge to that position, i.e.--- how could the Rapture have taken place prior to the completion of the New Testament in 95 A.D. We will address this matter [imminence] first because of the ease in which it can be scripturally dismissed.

The following are a few scriptural references commonly used to support the pre-tribulation rapture and the Doctrine of IMMINENCE:

Matthew 25:13-14

*13 Watch therefore, **for ye know neither the day nor the hour** wherein the Son of man cometh.*

It is claimed in the Doctrine of Imminence; that "not knowing the hour of Christ's coming" is tantamount to IMMINENCE.

Matthew 24:42-43

*42 Watch therefore: **for ye know not what hour** your Lord doth come.*

Matthew 24:44-45

*44 Therefore be ye also ready: for **in such an hour as ye think not** the Son of man cometh.*

Mark 13:32-33

*32 **But of that day and that hour knoweth no man**, no, not the angels which are in heaven, neither the Son, but the Father.*

1 Thessalonians 5:2-4

*2 For yourselves know perfectly that **the day of the Lord so cometh as a thief** in the night.*

It is emphatically held that because the phrase "coming as a thief" is used several times in the New Testament, that this phrase is also tantamount to Imminence.

3 For when they shall say, Peace and safety; then sudden destruction cometh upon them, as travail upon a woman with child; and they shall not escape.

2 Peter 3:10-11

*10 But the day of the Lord **will come as a thief in the night**; in the which the heavens shall pass away with a great noise, and the elements shall melt with fervent heat, the earth also and the works that are therein shall be burned up.*

Revelation 16:15-16

*15 **Behold, I come as a thief.** Blessed is he that watcheth, and keepeth his garments, lest he walk naked, and they see his shame.*

Kept From Wrath

2 Thessalonians 2:7-9

*7 For the mystery of iniquity doth already work: **only he who now letteth will let, until he be taken out of the way.***

It is proposed in this verse, that the reference to "he that now letteth" is none other than the Holy Spirit restraining antichrist from coming to power until he [the Holy Spirit] is removed from the earth, with the Church, in the Rapture. It is also believed that there has been an antichrist "waiting in the wings" throughout Church history so that he [Antichrist] can be revealed at any moment in time throughout the Church age. I will address the matter of the "restrainer" of II Thessalonians 2 later in this chapter.

8 And then shall that Wicked be revealed, whom the Lord shall consume with the spirit of his mouth, and shall destroy with the brightness of his coming:

2 Thessalonians 2:13-14

*13 But we are bound to give thanks alway to God for you, brethren beloved of the Lord, because God hath from the beginning **chosen*** *you to salvation through sanctification of the Spirit and belief of the truth:*

It is claimed in this verse, that the words "chosen you to salvation" supports the notion that the Church will be raptured prior to seven years of tribulation. It is also believed that the "seven years of tribulation" is synonymous with the "WRATH OF GOD".

<u>1 Thessalonians 5:9-10</u>

*9 For God hath **not appointed us to wrath**, but to obtain salvation by our Lord Jesus Christ,*

It is proposed that the word "Wrath" is tantamount to seven years of tribulation, though not supported in scripture.

<u>1 Peter 1:5-6</u>

*5 Who are **kept by the power of God through faith unto salvation** ready to be Revealed in the last time.*

It is said that this phrase supports the notion that the Church will be raptured before the seven years of tribulation begins.

<u>Revelation 3:10-11</u>

*10 Because thou hast kept the word of my patience, **I also will keep thee from the hour of temptation, which shall come upon all the world**, to try them that dwell upon the earth.*

Another contention is that the "seven years of tribulation" is synonymous to the "Wrath of God" and that the Church is exempt from that [implied] wrath.

<u>Revelation 4:1-3</u>

*4:1 After this I looked, and, behold, a door was opened in heaven: and the first voice which **I heard was as it were of a trumpet talking with me; which said, Come up hither**, and I will shew thee things which must be hereafter.*

2 And immediately I was in the spirit: and, behold, a throne was set in heaven, and one sat on the throne.

It is proposed that John the Revelator [in his vision] has been cast forth in time, to that point when the rapture has taken place. This, based on the phrase "come up hither" at the sound of a "voice as a trumpet".

Rapture Event

1 Corinthians 15:52-54

*52 In a moment, in the twinkling of an eye, at the last trump: for the trumpet shall sound, **and the dead shall be raised incorruptible, and we shall be changed.***

53 For this corruptible must put on incorruption, and this mortal must put on immortality.

1 Thessalonians 4:15-18

15 For this we say unto you by the word of the Lord, that we which are alive and remain unto the coming of the Lord shall not prevent them which are asleep.

16 For the Lord himself shall descend from heaven with a shout, with the voice of the archangel, and with the trump of God: and the dead in Christ shall rise first:

*17 **Then we which are alive and remain shall be caught up** together with them in the clouds, to meet the Lord in the air: and so shall we ever be with the Lord.*

It is proposed that these verses represent that "imminent rapture ". It is also believed that the rapture has been imminent since the Day of Pentecost just fifty days following the resurrection of Jesus.

No One Knows the Day Nor the Hour

Matthew 24:42:

"therefore, keep watch because you do not KNOW on what day your Lord will come"

It is taught in pre-tribulationism that these words of Jesus suggest an imminent rapture, and support the "coming as a THIEF" theory. Once again, we must look a little closer at the passage to understand the true meaning.

to "KNOW"

"KNOW" Strongs Reference # 1492: Greek – Iedo (eedo) to now know, always in the present "perfect" tense. As opposed to;

"KNOW" Strongs Reference # 1097: Greek – Ginosko (ghinoosko) "to perceive and understand."

In each and EVERY passage where it is declared "No man KNOWS the day nor the hour," the Greek word Iedo is used. It simply means---- "no man NOW KNOWS the day nor hour", it's that simple. Each and every time this phrase is used, it is ALWAYS attached to the clear admonition to WATCH for the signs of His coming. ALL THE SIGNS!!

In Matthew 24 (the Olivet Discourse), the command to watch for the signs of His (Jesus) coming, both PRECEED and FOLLOW (the statement "No man KNOWS (IEDO) the day nor hour". The Lord has made it emphatically clear, that we must KNOW (ginosko – to understand, to perceive) "the watch". A simple example is this: you're driving down a highway, there are no mile markers. You do not KNOW (IEDO) how much further to your destination until you see some identifiable markers saying "Kingdom City – 5 miles," then you begin to KNOW (iedo) some detail. As you drive further, you see a sign "Kingdom City – Next Exit, ¼ mile". Now you KNOW (iedo) even more, and so-on until you arrive at the corner of Matthew and 24th street where you make a right hand turn till you come to the crossing of 24th street and 30th Avenue. Now you KNOW (IEDO and Ginosko- perceive) where you are. This is exactly

7

what these passages say. You must ALWAYS weigh what is VAGUE in scripture, against what is EMPHATIC. "iedo" is the emphatic whereas "Ghinosko" is more vague. When you are confronted by this conflict, you MUST ALWAYS dig deeper. These things are NOT unknown to those educated in pre-tribulation theology. This makes them all the more accountable for their utterly false doctrine! Jesus declared to his disciples (and the Church of the Ages) – You do not NOW know [iedo], so you must watch for the signs, and as you BEGIN to see the signs, you will KNOW [ghinosko] that more and more signs are forth coming, and then suddenly you will arrive at that LAST SIGN preceding the gathering of the elect when "THE SUN BECOMES DARK as SACK CLOTH, THE MOON WILL NOT GIVE HER LIGHT, THE POWERS OF THE HEAVEN SHALL BE SHAKEN AND THE SIGN OF THE SON OF MAN, and He shall send His ANGELS to gather His elect from Heaven (the souls of the righteous dead) and earth (those who are alive and remain unto His coming)" Mark 13.

Mark 13:24-31:

*"²⁴But in those days, **after that tribulation, the sun shall be darkened, and the moon shall not give her light,***

²⁵And the stars of heaven shall fall, and the powers that are in heaven shall be shaken.

*²⁶**And then shall they see the Son of man coming in the clouds with great power and glory.***

*²⁷**And then shall he send his angels, and shall gather together his elect from the four winds, from the uttermost part of the earth to the uttermost part of heaven.***

²⁸Now learn a parable of the fig tree; When her branch is yet tender, and putteth forth leaves, ye know that summer is near:

*²⁹So ye in like manner, **when ye shall see these things come to pass, know [ginosko]** that it is nigh, even at the doors.*

³⁰Verily I say unto you, that this generation shall not pass, till all these things be done.

[31]Heaven and earth shall pass away: but my words shall not pass away."

I Thessalonians 4:13-17:

"[13]But I would not have you to be ignorant, brethren, **concerning them which are asleep,** that ye sorrow not, even as others which have no hope.

[14]For if we believe that Jesus died and rose again, **even so them also which sleep in Jesus will God bring with him.**

[15]For this we say unto you by the word of the Lord, that we which are alive and remain unto the coming of the Lord shall not prevent them which are asleep.

[16]For the Lord himself shall descend from heaven with a shout, with the voice of the archangel, and with the trump of God: and the dead in Christ shall rise first:

[17]**Then we which are alive and remain shall be caught up together with them in the clouds, to meet the Lord in the air:** and so shall we ever be with the Lord."

Blessed will be that day when the Union of "IEDO" and "GINOSKO" comes to pass, for THEN, the rapture will become ---- IMMINENT.

The Wrath Of God

Daniel 9:27-10:1

27 And he shall confirm the covenant with many for one week: and in the midst of the week he shall cause the sacrifice and the oblation to cease, and for the overspreading of abominations he shall make it desolate, even until the consummation, and that determined shall be poured upon the desolate.

Contrary to the historic understanding of this great passage, the pre-tribulationists claim that this passage is speaking of ANTICHRIST and the beginning of seven years of tribulation and that three and one half years into the tribulation, antichrist will abominate a newly rebuilt temple in Jerusalem, and trigger the beginning of the Great Tribulation----the final three and one half years of the "70th week of Daniel [tribulation]". This error is thoroughly discussed later in the book.

Revelation 6:1-3

6:1 And I saw when the Lamb opened one of the seals, and I heard, as it were the noise of thunder, one of the four beasts saying, Come and see.

*2 And I saw, and behold a white horse: **and he that sat on him had a bow**; and a crown was given unto him: and he went forth conquering, and to conquer.*

It is believed that this RIDER of a white horse is ANTICHRIST being released into the world----triggering seven years of tribulation though there is actually nothing in scripture to support this notion.

Common Beliefs About the Rapture

- ❖ It is imminent-------No necessary preceding signs or indicators. It has been immanent since Pentecost [50 days following the resurrection of Jesus].

- ❖ Antichrist will appear----A seven year "PEACE COVENANT" between Israel and her enemies will be signed immediately following the rapture. Antichrist will be the broker of that agreement.

- ❖ Billions of un-believers will be LEFT BEHIND to suffer the tribulation when the rapture takes place.

❖ 144,000 Jewish evangelists will cover the earth----some say to spread the Gospel----some say to condemn the earth, depending on one's belief as to whether or not people can be saved during the tribulation.

❖ The "ELECT" of Matthew 24 are Jews-----hence, a specific gathering of the Jews following the Great Tribulation.

❖ The "FIRST RESURRECTION" is a "PHASED EVENT" Revelation.20;4-7 is phase two of a three phase event. Phase one being the pre-tribulation rapture.

❖ The rapture has been imminent since Pentecost----just fifty days following the resurrection of Jesus.

❖ The rapture is a SILENT event and not related to the gathering event of Matthew 24. It is purported that Matthew 24 and Mark 13 hold little relevance to the Church. The passage speaks specifically to the Jews.

❖ The MARRIAGE SUPPER of the Lamb takes place in heaven soon after the rapture.

❖ The JUDGMENT SEAT of CHRIST takes place in heaven.

❖ The Church will be in heaven for SEVEN YEARS as the "wrath of God [tribulation]" is poured out on the earth.

❖ The "restrainer" of II Thes.2 is the CHURCH----indwelt by the Holy Spirit, and when the Church is raptured from the earth, the Holy Spirit will be removed as well.

❖ The PERPETUAL Man of Sin----an antichrist has been prepared throughout the Church age to accommodate an imminent rapture.

❖ The "Day of the Lord", and Christ's COMING as a thief, are NOT synonymous!

❖ II Thessalonians 2------- the "coming of the Lord", and "our gathering unto him", are TWO SEPARATE EVENTS which are separated in time by SEVEN YEARS

Imminence

John 21:18

[18] Verily, verily, I say unto thee, When thou wast young, thou girdedst thyself, and walkedst whither thou wouldest: but when thou shalt be old, thou shalt stretch forth thy hands, and another shall gird thee, and carry thee whither thou wouldest not.

In this passage; Jesus is prophesying the martyrdom of Peter. The passage follows by saying: "by this he spake of what manner of death that Peter should suffer". Let's look further:

II Peter 1:13-14

*[13]Yea, I think it meet, as long as I am in this tabernacle, to stir you up by putting you in remembrance; [14]Knowing that shortly I must put off this my tabernacle, **even as our Lord Jesus Christ hath shewed me.***

In preparing the Church for his soon departure; Peter reminds the Church of this prophecy that the Lord had given to him as a young man. Now Peter is far along in years, and the Lord has revealed to him that his final journey was at hand. It is very easy through this passage alone, to understand the impossibility of an imminent rapture in Peter's lifetime since the Lord himself had prophesied Peter's martyrdom in his elder years. How could the rapture have taken place prior to this prophetic event? I have heard such Bible teachers as Dr. David Jeremiah proclaim boldly that the Apostles believed in an imminent rapture. Obviously Dr. Jeremiah is wrong.

The next challenge comes in:

Acts 23:10-11

[10]And when there arose a great dissension, the chief captain, fearing lest Paul should have been pulled in pieces of them, commanded the soldiers to go down, and to take him by force from among them, and to bring him into the castle. [11]And the night following the Lord stood

by him, and said, Be of good cheer, Paul: for as thou hast testified
of me in Jerusalem, so must thou bear witness also at Rome.

In this passage, the Lord appears to Paul and assures him that
he [Jesus] is not through with him yet. Now the Lord tells him:"
YOU MUST PREACH THE GOSPEL IN ROME". It is quite impossible
that the rapture could have been imminent if Paul was told that
he [Paul], would PREACH THE GOSPEL IN ROME! Could Paul have
been raptured prior to his preaching the Gospel in Rome?

Looking further:

We know that the FIRST BOOK of the New Testament was
not penned until approximately THIRTY FIVE YEARS following
Pentecost. We know also that the Book of Revelation was not
penned until approximately 95 AD. Most would agree that it would
be quite LUDICROUS to believe that the RAPTURE was "imminent"
prior to the completion of the NEW TESTAMENT. Such a notion is
beyond any level of human reason. It cannot be entertained for
even a moment, yet some will cling to this absurdity simply in
regard to THE ELDERS [of pre-tribulationism], and THE TRADITIONS
OF MEN. It is amazing to me, that Christians will forsake the
strength of the New Testament, to cling to such monkey-play.
Jesus said "blessed is he who reads the words of this book-----
"Revelation". How was one to read the Book of Revelation--------
if he could have been been taken in an imminent rapture before
Revelation was written? This is insane theology.

HERE is the Lord's description of the Church Age:

Matthew 25:14-19

¹⁴For the kingdom of heaven is as a man travelling into a far country,
who called his own servants, and delivered unto them his goods.

¹⁵And unto one he gave five talents, to another two, and to another
one; to every man according to his several ability; and straightway
took his journey.

¹⁶*Then he that had received the five talents went and traded with the same, and made them other five talents.*

¹⁷*And likewise he that had received two, he also gained other two.*

¹⁸*But he that had received one went and digged in the earth, and hid his lord's money.*

¹⁹**After a long time** *the lord of those servants cometh, and reckoneth with them.*

The Lord says here that he will be gone "FOR A LONG TIME"-------how long is "A LONG TIME"?--------fifty days till Pentecost?----when the Church [as they say] could have been Raptured? Hardly likely.

How about this? Luke 21:24

²⁴*And they shall fall by the edge of the sword, and shall be led away captive into all nations: and Jerusalem shall be trodden down of the Gentiles,* ***until the times of the Gentiles be fulfilled.***

Jesus says that Jerusalem would be in the hands of the gentiles until the TIMES OF THE GENTILES are fulfilled. Could the Rapture have come before the "times of the gentiles" are fulfilled?

Paul tells the Thessalonian Church very clearly:

I Thessalonians 5:1-5

¹*But of the times and the seasons, brethren, ye have no need that I write unto you.* ²*For yourselves know perfectly that the day of the Lord so cometh as a thief in the night.* ³*For when they shall say, Peace and safety; then sudden destruction cometh upon them, as travail upon a woman with child; and they shall not escape.* ⁴***But ye, brethren, are not in darkness, that that day should overtake you as a thief.*** ⁵*Ye are all the children of light, and the children of the day: we are not of the night, nor of darkness.*

According to the Apostle Paul, We will NEVER BE TAKEN BY SURPRISE!

The Two Days of Hosea

Hosea 3:4-5

⁴For the children of Israel shall abide many days without a king, and without a prince, and without a sacrifice, and without an image, and without an ephod, and without teraphim:

*⁵**Afterward shall the children of Israel return, and seek the LORD** their God, **and David their king**; and shall fear the LORD and his goodness **in the latter days.***

Who can argue against this fantastic prophecy? The Lord speaks to the "children of Israel" with this wonderful prophecy. It speaks of the restoration of Israel in "the latter days". What does this great prophecy tell us about the Doctrine of Imminence, and the notion that the Church "could have been raptured" at any moment during the Church age?

Hosea 6:1-3

*¹**Come, and let us return unto the LORD**: for he hath torn, and he will heal us; he hath smitten, and he will bind us up.*

*²**After two days will he lift us up: in the third day he will raise us up, and we shall live in his sight.***

*³Then shall we know, **if we follow on to know the LORD**: his going forth is prepared as the morning; and he shall come unto us as the rain, as the latter and former rain unto the earth . . .*

This passage speaks of MILLINIAL DAYS. It could be NONE ELSE------After TWO millennial days he will return to Israel, and in the THIRD MILLINIAL DAY he will LIFT ISRAEL UP, and they shall live in his sight in the millennial reign of Christ. It has been nearly two millennia since Israel was "smitten", the third millennial [day] is just ahead. It is impossible that the rapture could take place prior to the "times of the gentiles" being fully accomplished.

Here's one that has been overlooked by millions in modern prophecy circles:

<u>Luke 10:30-35</u>

[30] And Jesus answering said, A certain man went down from Jerusalem to Jericho, and fell among thieves, which stripped him of his raiment, and wounded him, and departed, leaving him half dead.

[31] And by chance there came down a certain priest that way: and when he saw him, he passed by on the other side.

[32] And likewise a Levite, when he was at the place, came and looked on him, and passed by on the other side.

[33] But a certain Samaritan, as he journeyed, came where he was: and when he saw him, he had compassion on him,

[34] And went to him, and bound up his wounds, pouring in oil and wine, and set him on his own beast, and brought him to an inn, and took care of him.

[35] And on the morrow when he departed, **he took out two pence, and gave them to the host, and said unto him, Take care of him; and whatsoever thou spendest more, when I come again, I will repay thee**

In this type and foreshadow; the Samaritan [Christ], leaves the injured man [mankind] in the care of a keeper [the Church] and gives the keeper two pence---------TWO DAYS WAGES------and proclaims "When I COME AGAIN-----I WILL REPAY THEE" -------a wonderful reflection of the TWO DAYS OF HOSEA and Christ's return and our rewards with him at his coming.

Another pearl from the New Testament:

<u>John 6</u>

6 When he had heard therefore that he was sick, he abode **two days** still in the same place where he was

This speaks of the death of Lazarus, the Lord's dear friend. When Jesus was summoned by the family of Lazarus, HE ABODE TWO DAYS------WHY? I'll tell you why------

He [Christ] is the RESSURECTION AND THE LIFE------and THOUGH A MAN DIE-------YET SHALL HE LIVE!

Jesus waited TWO DAYS as a representation of the FIRST RESSURECTION after two millennial days. Many believe that Jesus waited TWO DAYS so that Lazarus would be "GOOD AND DEAD"------to give LEVERAGE to this miracle. NOT SO! He waited TWO DAYS as an act pointing to the Resurrection of the righteous---"after two days he will lift us up and in the third day we shall live in his sight" [Hosea].

If the rapture had come in the times of the Apostles.

Consider these events that would be missing from history in the event of a first century RAPTURE, followed by seven years of tribulation , followed by the Millennial reign of Christ as proposed in Pre-Trib theology.

- ❖ No canonization of the New Testament

- ❖ No invention of the printing press to enable the Gospel to go throughout the earth

- ❖ No REFORMATION

- ❖ No 1611 translation

- ❖ No Pilgrims

- ❖ No USA-----1776

- ❖ No Israel-----1948

- ❖ No Church Age

- ❖ No gentile age

- ❖ No wars, rumors of wars, earthquakes, famines

- ❖ **No SEVEN CHURCHES of the Church Age**

- ❖ **No Gospel preached in all the earth**

- ❖ **No you----and no me, who are chosen in him before the foundation of the earth.**

All of these events would never have occurred had the Church been RAPTURED prior to the opening of the Second Century, or any other day of the Church age. The DOCTRINE OF IMMINENCE is-----BLATANTLY FALSE!

Face the TRUTH

We have examined this doctrine from the point of human reason and discovered it to be absurd. Now we will focus more on the clarity of the pure Word of God.

The LAST DAY

John 6:39-45

*39 And this is the Father's will which hath sent me, that of all which he hath given me I should lose nothing, **but should raise it up again** at the last day.*

40 And this is the will of him that sent me, that every one which seeth the Son, and believeth on him, may have everlasting life: and I will raise him up at the last day.

41 The Jews then murmured at him, because he said, I am the bread which came down from heaven.

42 And they said, Is not this Jesus, the son of Joseph, whose father and mother we know? how is it then that he saith, I came down from heaven?

43 Jesus therefore answered and said unto them, Murmur not among yourselves.

*44 No man can come to me, except the Father which hath sent me draw him: **and I will raise him up at the last day***

John 6:54-55

*54 Whoso eateth my flesh, and drinketh my blood, hath eternal life; and **I will raise him up at the last day.***

What the saints under the OLD COVENANT believed

John 11:22-25

22 But I know, that even now, whatsoever thou wilt ask of God, God will give it thee.

23 Jesus saith unto her, Thy brother shall rise again.

*24 Martha saith unto him, I know that he shall rise again **in the resurrection at the last day.***

John 12:48-49

*48 He that rejecteth me, and receiveth not my words, hath one that judgeth him: the word that I have spoken, **the same shall judge him** in the last day.*

According to the word of God, there is no possibility of a "resurrection" until--------The LAST DAY! This alone eliminates any possibility of an imminent, Church Age Rapture!

Gone Missing?

In pre-tribulation theology it is said that "hundreds of millions of Christians will suddenly disappear in the "IMMINENT RAPTURE". Let's see how the Elect will be gathered according to the New Testament.

The Angels

Matthew 13:37-50

37 He answered and said unto them, He that soweth the good seed is the Son of man;

38 The field is the world; the good seed are the children of the kingdom; but the tares are the children of the wicked one;

39 The enemy that sowed them is the devil; **the harvest is the end of the world; and** the reapers are the angels.

40 As therefore the tares are gathered and burned in the fire; so shall **it be in the end of this world.**

41 The Son of man shall send forth his angels, and they shall gather out of his kingdom all things that offend, and them which do iniquity;

42 And shall cast them into a furnace of fire: there shall be wailing and gnashing of teeth.

43 Then shall the righteous shine forth as the sun in the kingdom of their Father. Who hath ears to hear, let him hear.

44 Again, the kingdom of heaven is like unto treasure hid in a field; the which when a man hath found, he hideth, and for joy thereof goeth and selleth all that he hath, and buyeth that field.

45 Again, the kingdom of heaven is like unto a merchant man, seeking goodly pearls:

46 Who, when he had found one pearl of great price, went and sold all that he had, and bought it.

47 Again, the kingdom of heaven is like unto a net, that was cast into the sea, and gathered of every kind:

48 Which, when it was full, they drew to shore, and sat down, and gathered the good into vessels, but cast the bad away.

49 **So shall it be at the end of the world: the angels shall come forth, and sever the wicked from among the just,**

Matthew 24:29-32

29 **Immediately after the tribulation of those days** shall the sun be darkened, and the moon shall not give her light, and the stars shall fall from heaven, and the powers of the heavens shall be shaken:

*30 **And then shall appear the sign of the Son of man in heaven:** and then shall all the tribes of the earth mourn, and they shall see the Son of man coming in the clouds of heaven with power and great glory.*

*31 **And he shall send his angels with a great sound of a trumpet, and they shall gather together his elect from the four winds, from one end of heaven to the other.***

Mark 13:24-28

*24 **But in those days, after that tribulation,** the sun shall be darkened, and the moon shall not give her light,*

25 And the stars of heaven shall fall, and the powers that are in heaven shall be shaken.

*26 **And then shall they see the Son of man coming in the clouds with great power and glory.***

*27 And then shall he send his angels, **and shall gather together his elect** from the four winds, from the uttermost part of the earth to the uttermost part of heaven.*

-------------------------------- *The SILENT RAPTURE*

It is commonly taught in this heretical position [THE DOCTRINE OF IMMINENCE], that the GATHERING [rapture] is a SILENT EVENT-----and will NOT be witnessed by the world. It is commonly declared that the ELECT will simply disappear at the sounding of a SILENT TRUMPET [some say] that only the Church can hear. It is said that the world will be mystified at this sudden phenomenon, and that the False Prophet will convince the world that that the Christians have been taken away from the earth by some Cosmic Deity so that the earth can be free of their influence. Others who have heard the Gospel, but rejected the call to Salvation, will crumble to their knees and weep bitterly because suddenly they realize that they have been LEFT BEHIND. It is taught that all the children of the world that are under the "age of accountability" will be taken in the secret SILENT RAPTURE. There are numerous other notions regarding this event that cannot be supported in scripture. Let's see what the New Testament says about the "SILENT RAPTURE".

21

COMING IN CLOUDS OF GLORY

Matthew 24:27-31

27 **For as the lightning cometh out of the east, and shineth even unto the west; so shall also the coming of the Son of man be.**

28 *For wheresoever the carcass is, there will the eagles be gathered together.*

29 *Immediately after the tribulation of those days shall the sun be darkened, and the moon shall not give her light, and the stars shall fall from heaven, and the powers of the heavens shall be shaken:*

30 *And then shall appear the sign of the Son of man in heaven: and then shall all the tribes of the earth mourn, and they shall see the Son of man* **coming in the clouds of heaven with power and great glory.**

Luke 21:25-29

25 *And there shall be signs in the sun, and in the moon, and in the stars; and upon the earth distress of nations, with perplexity; the sea and the waves roaring;*

26 *Men's hearts failing them for fear, and for looking after those things which are coming on the earth: for the powers of heaven shall be shaken.*

27 *And then shall they see the Son of man coming in a cloud with power and great glory.*

28 *And when these things begin to come to pass, then look up, and lift up your heads; for your redemption draweth nigh. 1 Thess 4:15-5:1* **15 For this we say unto you by the word of the Lord, that we which are alive and remain unto the coming of the Lord shall not prevent them which are asleep.16 For the Lord himself** *shall descend from heaven with a shout, with the voice of the* archangel, and with the trump of God: **and the dead in Christ shall rise first:**

17 Then we which are alive and remain shall be caught up together with them in the clouds, to meet the Lord in the air: and so shall we ever be with the Lord.

18 Wherefore comfort one another with these words.

The notion that the Rapture will be a "silent" event is preposterous, for every eye shall see him and HEAR THE TRUMPET. There is NOTHING in the DOCTRINE OF IMMINENCE that is scripturally wholesome. It is thoroughly CORRUPT. The preceding study is only a very SMALL portion of the mountain of evidence against this doctrine as we shall see.

TWO RESURRECTIONS

John 5:27-30

27 And hath given him authority to execute judgment also, because he is the Son of man.

28 Marvel not at this: for the hour is coming, in the which all that are in the graves shall hear his voice,

*29 And shall come forth; **they that have done good, unto the resurrection of life; and they that have done evil, unto the resurrection of damnation.***

John 11:23-25

23 Jesus saith unto her, Thy brother shall rise again.

*24 Martha saith unto him, **I know that he shall rise again in the resurrection at the last day.***

Luke 14:14-15

*14 And thou shalt be blessed; for they cannot recompense thee, **for thou shalt be recompensed at the resurrection of the just.***

Matthew 24:31

31 And he shall send his angels with a great sound of a trumpet, and they shall gather together his elect from the four winds, from one end of heaven to the other.

Acts 24:15-16

15 And have hope toward God, which they themselves also allow, that there shall be a resurrection of the dead, both of the just and unjust.

1 Thess 4:16-5:1

*16 For the Lord himself shall descend from heaven with a shout, with the voice of the archangel, **and with the trump of God: and the dead in Christ shall rise first:***

17 Then we which are alive and remain shall be caught up together with them in the clouds, to meet the Lord in the air: and so shall we ever be with the Lord.

18 Wherefore comfort one another with these words.

1 Corinthians 15:52-55

*52 In a moment, in the twinkling of an eye, **at the last trump**: for the trumpet shall sound, **and the dead shall be raised incorruption**, and we shall be changed.*

53 For this corruptible must put on incorruption, and this mortal must put on immortality.

54 So when this corruptible shall have put on incorruption, and this mortal shall have put on immortality, then shall be brought to pass the saying that is written, Death is swallowed up in victory.

Revelation 11:15-12:1

*15 And the **seventh angel sounded**; and there were great voices in heaven, saying, The kingdoms of this world are become the kingdoms of our Lord, and of his Christ; and he shall reign forever and ever.*

16 And the four and twenty elders, which sat before God on their seats, fell upon their faces, and worshipped God,

17 Saying, We give thee thanks, O Lord God Almighty, which art, and wast, and art to come; because thou hast taken to thee thy great power, and hast reigned.

*18 And the nations were angry, and thy wrath is come, and the time of the dead, that they should be judged, and that thou **shouldest give reward unto thy servants the prophets, and to the saints, and them that fear thy name, small and great; and shouldest destroy them which destroy the earth.***

19 And the temple of God was opened in heaven, and there was seen in his temple the ark of his testament: and there were lightnings, and voices, and thunderings, and an earthquake, and great hail.

Revelation 20:4-7

*4 And I saw thrones, and they sat upon them, and judgment was given unto them: **and I saw the souls of them that were beheaded for the witness of Jesus, and for the word of God, and which had not worshipped the beast, neither his image, neither had received his mark upon their foreheads,** or in their hands; and they lived and reigned with Christ a thousand years.*

*5 But the rest of the dead lived not again until the thousand years were finished. **This is the first resurrection.***

6 Blessed and holy is he that hath part in the first resurrection: on such the second death hath no power, but they shall be priests of God and of Christ, and shall reign with him a thousand years.

It is abundantly clear that there are only TWO resurrections, one of the righteous, and one of the unrighteous. Revelation 20:4-7 tells us specifically that the FIRST RESURRECTION will take place following the martyrdom of the Saints of the Great Tribulation. To deny such in the face of this preponderance of truth is tantamount to REBELLION. The SECOND resurrection will take place at the end of the millennial reign of Christ.

The LAST TRUMP

Matthew 24:31

*31 And he shall send his angels **with a great sound of a trumpet,** and they shall gather together his elect from the four winds, from one end of heaven to the other.*

1 Thess 4:16-5:1

*16 For the Lord himself shall descend from heaven with a shout, with the voice of the archangel, and **with the trump of God: and the dead in Christ shall rise first:***

17 Then we which are alive and remain shall be caught up together with them in the clouds, to meet the Lord in the air: and so shall we ever be with the Lord.

1 Corinthians 15:52

*52 In a moment, in the twinkling of an eye, **at the last trump:** for the trumpet shall sound, and the dead shall be raised incorruptible, **and we shall be changed.***

Revelation 11:15-18

*__15 And the seventh angel sounded;__ and there were great voices in heaven, saying, The kingdoms of this world are become the kingdoms of our Lord, and of his Christ; **and he shall reign forever and ever.***

16 And the four and twenty elders, which sat before God on their seats, fell upon their faces, and worshipped God,

17 Saying, We give thee thanks, O Lord God Almighty, which art, and wast, and art to come; because thou hast taken to thee thy great power, and hast reigned.

*18 And the nations were angry, and thy wrath is come, **and the time of the dead, that they should be judged, and that thou shouldest give reward unto thy servants the prophets, and to the saints, and them that fear thy name, small and great; and shouldest destroy them which destroy the earth.***

The New Testament is emphatic regarding its claim that the righteous dead will be raised AT THE LAST TRUMP and not before. Revelation 15 opens with these words----"And the seventh angel sounded". This is unquestionably the LAST TRUMP. There are no others to follow. It is the time of the Resurrection of the saints. Assuming that this is true, where does that place the Church at the sounding of trumpets ONE thru SIX, since the dead are raised FIRST-----at the LAST TRUMP?

Considering Revelation 11:8

1. it is the time of the dead that they should be judged

2. and time for the rewards of the Saints

3. and the time to destroy them that destroy the earth

It is clearly the resurrection of the dead at the TIME OF CHRIST'S RETURN----at the sounding of----THE LAST TRUMP!

About The END?

Matthew 10:22-23

22 And ye shall be hated of all men for my name's sake: **but he that endureth to the end shall be saved.**

Matthew 13:40-51

40 As therefore the tares are gathered and burned in the fire; **so shall it be in the end of this world.**

41 **The Son of man shall send forth his angels, and they shall gather out of his kingdom all things that offend, and them which do iniquity;**

42 And shall cast them into a furnace of fire: there shall be wailing and gnashing of teeth.

43 **Then shall the righteous shine forth as the sun in the kingdom of their Father. Who hath ears to hear, let him hear.**

44 Again, the kingdom of heaven is like unto treasure hid in a field; the which when a man hath found, he hideth, and for joy thereof goeth and selleth all that he hath, and buyeth that field.

45 Again, the kingdom of heaven is like unto a merchant man, seeking goodly pearls:

46 Who, when he had found one pearl of great price, went and sold all that he had, and bought it.

47 Again, the kingdom of heaven is like unto a net, that was cast into the sea, and gathered of every kind:

48 Which, when it was full, they drew to shore, and sat down, **and gathered the good into vessels, but cast the bad away.**

49 **So shall it be at the end of the world: the angels shall come forth, and sever the wicked from among the just,**

50 And shall cast them into the furnace of fire: there shall be wailing and gnashing of teeth. And ye shall hear of wars and rumours of wars: **see that ye be not troubled: for all these things must come to pass.**

Matthew 24;6-14

6 for ye shall hear of wars and rumors of wars, **but the end is not yet.**

7 For nation shall rise against nation, and kingdom against kingdom: and there shall be famines, and pestilences, and earthquakes, in divers places.

8 **All these are the beginning of sorrows.**

9 Then shall they deliver you up to be afflicted, and shall kill you: and ye shall be hated of all nations for my name's sake.

10 And then shall many be offended, and shall betray one another, and shall hate one another.

11 And many false prophets shall rise, and shall deceive many.

12 And because iniquity shall abound, the love of many shall wax cold.

*13 **But he that shall endure unto the end,** the same shall be saved.*

*14 And this gospel of the kingdom shall be preached in all the world for a witness unto all nations; **and then shall the end come.***

Matthew 28:20

*20 Teaching them to observe all things whatsoever I have commanded you: and, lo, **I am with you alway, even unto the end of the world. Amen.***

Mark 13:7-8

*7 And when ye shall hear of wars and rumours of wars, be ye not troubled: for such things must needs be; **but the end shall not be yet.***

Mark 13:13-14

*13 And ye shall be hated of all men for my name's sake: but **he that shall endure unto the end, the same shall be saved.***

Luke 21:9-10

*9 But when ye shall hear of wars and commotions, be not terrified: for these things must first come to pass; **but the end is not by and by.***

1 Corinthians 1:8-9

*8 **Who shall also confirm you unto the end,** that ye may be blameless in the day of our Lord Jesus Christ.*

1 Corinthians 15:23-25

*23 But every man in his own order: Christ the firstfruits; afterward they that are **Christ's at his coming.***

24 Then cometh the end, *when he shall have delivered up the kingdom to God, even the Father;* **when he shall have put down all rule and all authority and power.**

2 Corinthians 1:12-15

12 For our rejoicing is this, the testimony of our conscience, that in simplicity and godly sincerity, not with fleshly wisdom, but by the grace of God, we have had our conversation in the world, and more abundantly to you-ward.

13 For we write none other things unto you, than what ye read or acknowledge; and I trust ye shall acknowledge **even to the end;**

14 As also ye have acknowledged us in part, that we are your rejoicing, even as ye also are ours **in the day of the Lord Jesus.** *[cross reference to II Thess.2;1]*

1 Thess 3:13

God, even our Father, **at the coming of our Lord Jesus Christ with all his saints.**------*[the souls of righteous dead]*

1 Thess 3:13

13 **To the end he may stablish your hearts** *unblameable in holiness before God, even our Father,* **at the coming of our Lord Jesus Christ with all his saints [the souls of the righteous dead].**

Heb 3:6-7 6 But Christ as a son over his own house; whose house are we, if we hold fast the confidence and the rejoicing of the hope **firm unto the end.**

Heb 3:14-15

14 For we are made partakers of Christ, **if we hold the beginning of our confidence stedfast unto the end;**

Heb 6:11-12

11 And we desire that every one of you do shew the same diligence to the full assurance of hope **unto the end:**

1 Peter 1:9-14

9 Receiving the end of your faith, even the salvation of your souls.

10 Of which salvation the prophets have inquired and searched diligently, who prophesied of the grace that should come unto you:

11 Searching what, or what manner of time the Spirit of Christ which was in them did signify, when it testified beforehand the sufferings of Christ, and the glory that should follow.

12 Unto whom it was revealed, that not unto themselves, but unto us they did minister the things, which are now reported unto you by them that have preached the gospel unto you with the Holy Ghost sent down from heaven; which things the angels desire to look into.

*13 Wherefore gird up the loins of your mind, be sober, **and hope to the end** for the grace that is to be brought unto you **at the Revelation of Jesus Christ;***

Revelation 2:26-28

*26 **And he that overcometh, and keepeth my works unto the end,** to him will I give power over the nations:*

*27 **And he shall rule them with a rod of iron**; as the vessels of a potter shall they be broken to shivers: even as I received of my Father.*

HE THAT OVERCOMES

NT:----"overcome"

nikao (nik-ah'-o); from NT:3529; to subdue (literally or figuratively):

KJV - conquer, overcome, prevail, get the victory.

Danny McDowell

1 John 5:4-6

*4 For whatsoever is born of God **overcometh the world**: and this is the victory that overcometh the world, even our faith.*

*5 Who is he that **overcometh the world**, but he that believeth that Jesus is the Son of God?*

Revelation 2:7-8

*7 He that hath an ear, let him hear what the Spirit saith unto the churches; **To him that overcometh** will I give to eat of the tree of life, which is in the midst of the paradise of God.*

Revelation 2:11-12

*11 He that hath an ear, let him hear what the Spirit saith unto the churches; **He that overcometh shall not be hurt of the second death.***

Revelation 2:17-18

*17 He that hath an ear, let him hear what the Spirit saith unto the churches; **To him that overcometh** will I give to eat of the hidden manna, and will give him a white stone, and in the stone a new name written, which no man knoweth saving he that receiveth it.*

Revelation 2:26-27

*26 And **he that overcometh, and keepeth my works unto the end**, to him will I give power over the nations:*

Revelation 3:5-6

*5 **He that overcometh, the same shall be clothed in white raiment;** and I will not blot out his name out of the book of life, but I will confess his name before my Father, and before his angels. [White Raiment---**Revelation 7:9-14 these are those that came out of GREAT TRIBULATION]***

Revelation 3:12-13

*12 **Him that overcometh will I make a pillar in the temple of my God**, and he shall go no more out: and I will write upon him the name of my God, and the name of the city of my God, which is new Jerusalem, which cometh down out of heaven from my God: and I will write upon him my new name.*

Revelation 3:21-4:1

*21To **him that overcometh will I grant to sit with me in my throne**., even as I also overcame, and am set down with my Father in his throne. 22 He that hath an ear, let him hear what the Spirit saith unto the churches.*

Revelation 21:7-9

*7 **He that overcometh shall inherit all things**; and I will be his God, and he shall be my son.*

8 But the fearful, and unbelieving, and the abominable, and murderers, and whoremongers, and sorcerers, and idolaters, and all liars, shall have their part in the lake which burneth with fire and brimstone: which is the second death.

He That Endures

NT:5278----"endure"

hupomeno (hoop-om-en'-o); from NT:5259 and NT:3306; to stay under (behind), i.e. remain; figuratively, to undergo, i.e. bear (trials), have fortitude, persevere:

KJV - abide, endure, (take) patient (-ly), suffer, tarry behind.

Matthew 10:22-23

*22 And ye shall be hated of all men for my name's sake: **but he that endureth to the end shall be saved**.*

Matthew 24:13-15

13 **But he that shall endure unto the end, the same shall be saved.**

14 *And this gospel of the kingdom shall be preached in all the world for a witness unto all nations; and then shall the end come.*

Mark 13:13-14

13 *And ye shall be hated of all men for my name's sake: but he that shall* **endure unto the end, the same shall be saved.**

There is absolutely NO misunderstanding of this great volume of verses. Christians, we will be called upon to endure to the end of the age!-----the GENTILE AGE! Keeping this in mind, how can it be possible that the Church could have been RAPTURED at any given moment during the Church Age? It doesn't take a great theologian to figure this thing out. A CHILD with a sixth grade reading level can clearly understand these well defined declarations regarding the END OF THE AGE.

You may become bored with my laboring this point. My intention is to leave no question unanswered regarding this matter of the Gathering of God's Elect. The New Testament calls this "our blessed hope and glorious appearing of Jesus". It should not be trivialized as "ONE MAN'S OPINION verses another", nor any other shallow excuse for ignoring the truth. Church doctrine is no "coin flip". It's not a matter of "choices". We cannot simply "agree to disagree". It's a matter of TRUTH-----not MY TRUTH------not YOUR TRUTH-----just TRUTH!

Too Much to Lose

There are many proponents of the pre-tribulation Rapture who emphatically declare that the Rapture will be a SILENT EVENT. The rationale for this rather bizarre notion is based in their belief that the rather NOISY events of Matthew 24 take place seven years after the pre-trib "rapture" which triggers seven years of tribulation on the earth. In other words, they flatly dismiss the "GATHERING" of Matthew 24 as being the Rapture because the passage clearly states "immediately AFTER the tribulation of those days" the Son of man will gather his elect with the sounding of a great trumpet. These words of Matthew 24 stand at stark opposition to the Doctrine of imminence and the pre-tribulation Rapture. The entire discourse of Matthew 24 flies in the face of anything proposed in pre-trib theology. In other words, they establish their position----then dismiss the preponderance of Biblical evidence stacked against them for the sake of their corrupt doctrine, no matter how violent to exegesis. This is of little concern to the pre-tribulationist, for his GOAL is to "defend and further establish his doctrine" at any cost. Literally hundreds of millions of dollars have been made selling pre-trib books, study materials, and even a wildly popular book series [Left Behind]. It is far too late for them to change their minds----there is simply TOO MUCH VESTED----TOO MUCH TO LOSE at this point. It is just too difficult for Church leaders to stand in the pulpit and declare that ALL THEY HAVE PREVIOUSLY TAUGHT ABOUT THE RAPTURE IS WRONG. It is a matter of personal pride-----fleshly pride.

So now we are STUCK with THREE trumpet "arrivals" of Jesus. We have the pre-tribulation [silent] trumpet, the trumpets of Paul the Apostle [I Corinthians.15:52 and I Thess.4:16] which are in no way silent, and Revelation. 11:15 [the seventh trumpet] in which the context declares it to follow the previous six trumpets. There is only ONE TRUMPET that will sound at Christ's return. It is the SEVENTH TRUMPET of the book of Revelation ----It is the LAST TRUMP.

The Appearing

It's really important to actually READ each and every scripture verse presented in this work. It will ground you in amazing truth. You will soon come to a place where you will be convinced of the level of deception that you, myself, and others, even millions have succumbed to. This revelation regarding the "truth about the rapture" is only the opening salvo in this war against Heresy, false doctrine, and apostasy. And now, on to THE APPEARING.

Col 3:3-5

3 For ye are dead, and your life is hid with Christ in God.

*4 When Christ, who is our life, **shall appear**, then shall ye also appear with him in glory.*

1 Peter 5:2-5

2 Feed the flock of God which is among you, taking the oversight thereof, not by constraint, but willingly; not for filthy lucre, but of a ready mind;

3 Neither as being lords over God's heritage, but being ensamples to the flock.

*4 And when the chief Shepherd **shall appear**, ye shall receive a crown of glory that fadeth not away.*

1 John 2:28-29

*28 And now, little children, abide in him; that, **when he shall appear**, we may have confidence, and not be ashamed before him **at his coming**.*

1 John 3:2-3

*2 Beloved, now are we the sons of God, and it doth not yet appear what we shall be: but we know that, **when he shall appear**, we shall be like him; for we shall see him as he is.*

2 Tim 4:1-5

*4:1 I charge thee therefore before God, and the Lord Jesus Christ, who shall judge the quick and the dead **at his appearing** and his kingdom;*

2 Preach the word; be instant in season, out of season; reprove, rebuke, exhort with all longsuffering and doctrine.

3 For the time will come when they will not endure sound doctrine; but after their own lusts shall they heap to themselves teachers, having itching ears;

*4 And they shall turn away their ears from the truth, **and shall be turned unto fables.***

2 Tim 4:7-9

7 I have fought a good fight, I have finished my course, I have kept the faith:

*8 Henceforth there is laid up for me a crown of righteousness, which the Lord, the righteous judge, shall give me **at that day**: and not to me only, **but unto all them also that love his appearing.***

Titus 2:13-14

*13 Looking for that blessed hope, and the **glorious appearing** of the great God and our Saviour Jesus Christ;*

1 Peter 1:7-8

*7 That the trial of your faith, being much more precious than of gold that perisheth, though it be tried with fire, might be found unto praise and honour and glory **at the appearing of Jesus Christ**:*

THE COMING

1 Corinthians 1:7-9

7 So that ye come behind in no gift; waiting for the coming of our Lord Jesus Christ:

*8 Who shall also confirm you **unto the end**, that ye may be blameless **in the day of our Lord Jesus Christ.***

1 Corinthians 15:23-25

*23 But every man in his own order: Christ the firstfruits; afterward **they that are Christ's at his coming.***

*24 **Then cometh the end**, when he shall have delivered up the kingdom to God, even the Father; when he shall have put down all rule and all authority and power.*

1 Thess 2:19-20

*19 For what is our hope, or joy, or crown of rejoicing? Are not even ye in the presence of our Lord Jesus Christ **at his coming**?*

1 Thess 4:15-5:1

*15 For this we say unto you by the word of the Lord, that we which are alive and remain **unto the coming of the Lord** shall not prevent them which are asleep.*

*16 For the Lord himself shall descend from heaven with a shout, with the voice of the archangel, and with the trump of God: **and the dead in Christ shall rise first**: [Revelation.20:4-7 **This is the first resurrection**].*

17 Then we which are alive and remain shall be caught up together with them in the clouds, to meet the Lord in the air: and so shall we ever be with the Lord.

18 Wherefore comfort one another with these words.

2 Thess 2:1-3

*2:1 Now we beseech you, brethren, **by the coming of our Lord Jesus Christ, and by our gathering together unto him**,*

*2 That ye be not soon shaken in mind, or be troubled, neither by spirit, nor by word, nor by letter as from us, **as that the day of Christ is at hand [imminent]**.*

2 Thess 2:8-10

*8 And then shall that Wicked be revealed, whom the Lord shall consume with the spirit of his mouth, and shall destroy **with the brightness of his coming**:*

9 Even him, whose coming is after the working of Satan with all power and signs and lying wonders,

<u>James 5:7-8</u>

*7 Be patient therefore, brethren, **unto the coming of the Lord**. Behold, the husbandman waiteth for the precious fruit of the earth, and hath long patience for it, until he receive the early **and later rain**.*

<u>II Peter 3:12-13</u>

*12 Looking for and hasting **unto the coming of the day of God,** wherein the heavens being on fire shall be dissolved, and the elements shall melt with fervent heat?*

<u>1 John 2:28-29</u>

*28 And now, little children, abide in him; that, **when he shall appear,** we may have confidence, **and not be ashamed before him at his coming**.*

Matt 16:27

27 For the Son of man shall come in the glory of his Father with his angels; **and then he shall reward every man according to his works**. KJV

We shall receive our crown AT HIS APPEARING and his Kingdom. We will be changed into immortality WHEN WE SEE HIM. This is our GLORIOUS HOPE. Those who teach pre-tribulationism would have us believe that there are TWO "comings" of Christ, the FIRST being prior to the opening of "seven years of Tribulation", and the SECOND return of Christ at the end of the Great Tribulation. They use the BIBLICAL word "coming" interchangeably to suit their particular motive. One "coming" represents the pre-tribulation Rapture, the other "coming" represents the return of Christ to set up his Kingdom on earth. The fact is----there is only ONE "coming" as clearly revealed in these previous scripture verses.

The DAY of THE LORD---- THE WRATH OF GOD

Pre-tribulationism has but one view concerning the "Wrath of God." That view declares emphatically that the entire 70th week of Daniel (7 years of tribulation) and the "Wrath of God" are synonymous. Furthermore, since the church has been promised exclusion from God's wrath [The 70th week of Daniel], the church must therefore be gathered prior to the opening of that event - hence "The Pre-Tribulation Rapture!" Some verses used to undergird this position are:

I Thessalonians 5:9

"⁹For God hath not appointed us to wrath, but to obtain salvation by our Lord Jesus Christ,"

. . . Since the 70th week of Daniel and the "Wrath of God" are considered synonymous in Pre-Trib theology, it is believed impossible for the church to enter the 70th week of Daniel (7 years of tribulation), since we are not "appointed to God's wrath".

The Restrainer

II Thessalonians 2:6-8

"⁶And now ye know what withholdeth that he might be revealed in his time.

⁷For the mystery of iniquity doth already work: only he who now letteth will let, until he be taken out of the way.

⁸And then shall that Wicked be revealed, whom the Lord shall consume with the spirit of his mouth, and shall destroy with the brightness of his coming:"

. . . It is said in Pre-Tribulation doctrine, that the "restraining force" spoken of in this passage is "The Church, indwelt by the Holy Spirit" and that this "Restraining influence" will be removed from the earth [at the rapture] prior to 7 years of tribulation, even though there is no evidence in scripture that supports the contention that the "restrainer" of II Thessalonians 2 is none other than the Holy Spirit. Even the modern day fathers of pre-tribulationism [Ryrie and Pentecost] confess that their appointment of the Holy Spirit to that post of II Thessalonians 2:7 is CONJECTURE. Conjecture is not necessary when there is clear scriptural validation to the identity of the "restrainer" of II Thessalonians 2. Again----we must never exchange the "absolute" for the "circumstantial". We will discuss the "restrainer of II Thessalonians 2 later in this chapter.

II Thessalonians 2:13

*"¹³But we are bound to give thanks alway to God for you, brethren beloved of the Lord, because God hath from the beginning **chosen you to salvation** through sanctification of the Spirit and belief of the truth:"*

... This verse is commonly used to support II Thessalonians 2:6-8. It is said that the phrase "has appointed you to salvation," indicates salvation from the "7 years of tribulation".

Revelation 3:18

*"¹⁰Because thou hast kept the word of my patience, I also will **KEEP THEE** from the hour of temptation, which shall come upon all the world, to try them that dwell upon the earth."*

... It is said that the phrase "I also will keep thee from the hour of temptation "is referring to the 7 years previously mentioned.

Revelation 4:1

*"¹After this I looked, and, behold, a door was opened in heaven: and the first voice **which I heard was as it were of a trumpet talking with me;** which said, **Come up hither,** and I will show thee things which must be hereafter."*

... It is said that because John heard "a voice as a trumpet" and saw "a door was opened in heaven," that he was thrust forward in time and translated WITH THE CHURCH at the pre-trib rapture. It is also proposed, because Revelation 4:1 precedes the Revelation of "Antichrist" in Revelation 6, that this is substantial evidence of a pre-tribulation rapture. The fact is completely ignored that it is NOT the "voice of a trumpet" that summons God's elect, but an actual "TRUMPET"----the LAST TRUMP.

NT:4536----trumpet-----last trump

salpigx (sal'-pinx); perhaps from NT:4535 (through the idea of quavering or reverberation):

KJV - a trumpet:

KJV - trump (-et).

This TRUMPET will shake the earth with reverberation. There has never been a trumpet like this GREAT TRUMPET. Noting that JOHN was taken through an "OPEN DOOR" in heaven [Rev.4:1], disqualifies this experience as representing the rapture----for we shall not be called up through an "open door", but we shall meet Christ IN THE AIR!

Let's see what the Bible has to say about, The Wrath of God ,

The Day of The Lord

It is fanatically held in PRE-TRIBULATION doctrine that the "Day of The Lord" and the 70th week of Daniel [7 years of tribulation] are synonymous, and since the church of all ages has been promised exclusion from God's Wrath, the church will be taken out of the earth prior to the terrible events of the Tribulation.

It seems logical to me, that to SPECIFICALLY IDENTIFY the "Day of the Lord" is critical to any eschatological position regarding the rapture. There is NOT a scrap of evidence anywhere in the Bible that will connect the entirety of the 70th week of Daniel (7 years of tribulation) to the "Day of The Lord"! So much of pre-tribulation reasoning depends on this single issue. I therefore challenge ANYONE to biblically connect the 70th week in part, or in its entirety, to the "Day of The Lord". Once again, I must say "Nothing in scripture connects "7 years of tribulation" to the Biblical "DAY OF THE LORD"! In fact, the DAY OF THE LORD has some very unique identifying markers which are not contained within the narrative posed in Matthew 24 [the Olivette Discourse], other than those markers which are pronounced as "immediately AFTER the tribulation of those days".

It is said in pre-tribulation theology that the 7 years of tribulation begins with the signing of a "PEACE COVENANT" between Anti-

Christ and other nations for the safety and protection of Israel. Many believe that this political agreement will provide for the construction of the 3rd Temple on Mount Moriah in Jerusalem. Let's look to the scriptures to find out how THE DAY OF THE LORD begins.

Isaiah 2:10-22

"10Enter into the rock, and hide thee in the dust, for fear of the LORD, and for the glory of his majesty.

11The lofty looks of man shall be humbled, and the haughtiness of men shall be bowed down, and the LORD alone shall be exalted in that day.

12For the day of the LORD of hosts shall be upon every one that is proud and lofty, and upon every one that is lifted up; and he shall be brought low:

13And upon all the cedars of Lebanon, that are high and lifted up, and upon all the oaks of Bashan,

14And upon all the high mountains, and upon all the hills that are lifted up, 15And upon every high tower, and upon every fenced wall,

16And upon all the ships of Tarshish, and upon all pleasant pictures.

17And the loftiness of man shall be bowed down, and the haughtiness of men shall be made low: and the LORD alone shall be exalted in that day.

18And the idols he shall utterly abolish.

19And they shall go into the holes of the rocks, and into the caves of the earth, for fear of the LORD, and for the glory of his majesty, when he ariseth to shake terribly the earth.

20In that day a man shall cast his idols of silver, and his idols of gold, which they made each one for himself to worship, to the moles and to the bats;

²¹*To go into the clefts of the rocks, and into the tops of the ragged rocks, for fear of the LORD, and for the glory of his majesty, when he ariseth to shake terribly the earth.*

²²*Cease ye from man, whose breath is in his nostrils: for wherein is he to be accounted of?"*

Verse 10:

*"¹⁰Enter into the rock, **and hide thee in the dust, for fear of the LORD**, and for the glory of his majesty."*

❖ **Men enter into the rocks to hide from the Lord [Revelation 6:15-16].**

Verse 11:

*"¹¹The lofty looks of man shall be humbled, and the haughtiness of men shall be bowed down, **and the LORD alone shall be exalted in that day.**"*

❖ **Man shall be humbled, ALL MEN----including antichrist!**

Verse 12:

*"¹²**For the day of the LORD of hosts shall be upon every one that is proud and lofty,** and upon every one that is lifted up; and he shall be brought low:"*

❖ **Does this describe Antichrist----"proud and lofty"?**

Verse 13-16:

"¹³And upon all the cedars of Lebanon, that are high and lifted up, and upon all the oaks of Bashan, ¹⁴And upon all the high mountains, and upon all the hills that are lifted up, ¹⁵And upon every high tower, and upon every fenced wall, ¹⁶And upon all the ships of Tarshish, and upon all pleasant pictures."

❖ **Everything and every person will be humbled in the Day of The LORD!**

Verse 17:

*"¹⁷And the loftiness of man shall be bowed down, and the haughtiness of men shall be made low: **and the LORD alone shall be exalted in that day.**"*

❖ **"THE LORD ALONE"** will be exalted in that day. Where does Anti-Christ and seven years of tribulation fit into this picture?

Verse 18:

"¹⁸And the idols he shall utterly abolish."

❖ All idols will be **UTTERLY ABOLISHED** in the **DAY** of the **LORD**. So much for the **IMAGE** of the **BEAST!**

Verse 19:

*"¹⁹**And they shall go into the holes of the rocks, and into the caves of the earth, for fear of the LORD,** and for the glory of his majesty, when he ariseth to shake terribly the earth."*

❖ Think they might be hiding from someone? [Revelation 6:15-16]?

Verse 21:

*"²¹**To go into the clefts of the rocks,** and into the tops of the ragged rocks, **for fear of the LORD,** and for the glory of his majesty, when he ariseth **to shake terribly the earth.**"*

❖ **WHO** is shaking the earth here? Is it antichrist, or God almighty?

Verse 22:

"²²Cease ye from man, whose breath is in his nostrils: for wherein is he to be accounted of?"

❖ **CEASE YE FROM MAN WHOSE BREATH IS IN HIS NOSTRILS FOR WHEREIN IS HE TO BE ACCOUNTED OF?** Could this include Anti-Christ?

<u>Isaiah 13:6-13</u>

*"⁶Howl ye; for the day of the LORD is at hand; **it shall come as a destruction from the Almighty.***

*⁷****Therefore shall all hands be faint, and every man's heart shall melt:***

⁸And they shall be afraid: pangs and sorrows shall take hold of them; they shall be in pain as a woman that travaileth: they shall be amazed one at another; their faces shall be as flames.

⁹Behold, the day of the LORD cometh, cruel both with wrath and fierce anger, to lay the land desolate: and he shall destroy the sinners thereof out of it.

*¹⁰****For the stars of heaven and the constellations thereof shall not give their light: the sun shall be darkened in his going forth, and the moon shall not cause her light to shine.***

*¹¹****And I will punish the world for their evil, and the wicked for their iniquity; and I will cause the arrogancy of the proud to cease, and will lay low the haughtiness of the terrible****.*

¹²I will make a man more precious than fine gold; even a man than the golden wedge of Ophir. ¹³Therefore I will shake the heavens, and the earth shall remove out of her place, in the wrath of the LORD of hosts, and in the day of his fierce anger."

Verse 6:

*"⁶Howl ye; for the day of the LORD is at hand; **it shall come as a destruction from the Almighty**."*

> ❖ **Where does the Day of the Lord come from in this verse? [Isaiah 2:17, Revelation 6:16-17] . Is Anti-Christ involved here?**

Verse 9:

*"⁹Behold, the day of the LORD cometh, cruel both with wrath and fierce anger, to lay the land desolate: **and he shall destroy the sinners thereof** out of it."*

❖ **Who gets destroyed here? Is Antichrist a sinner?**

Verse 10:

"¹⁰For the stars of heaven and the constellations thereof shall not give their light: the sun shall be darkened in his going forth, and the moon shall not cause her light to shine."

> ❖ **Hmm - the Sun and Moon are darkened. Have I read this somewhere else [Matthew. 24, Revelation.6]?**

Verse 11:

"¹¹And I will punish the world for their evil, and the wicked for their iniquity; and I will cause the arrogancy of the proud to cease, and will lay low the haughtiness of the terrible."

> ❖ **He will cause the arrogancy of the proud to cease [Isaiah 2:13-16].**

Verse 13:

*"¹³Therefore I will shake the heavens, and the earth shall remove out of her place, **in the wrath of the LORD of hosts**, and in the day of his fierce anger."*

> ❖ **Please, tell me, is this THE WRATH OF GOD?**

Joel 1:15

"¹⁵Alas for the day! for the day of the LORD is at hand, and as a destruction from the Almighty shall it come."

> ❖ **Again now, where does this wrath come from? Is Anti-Christ in any way involved in God's Wrath?**

Joel 2:1-2;

*"¹Blow ye the trumpet in Zion, and sound an alarm in my holy mountain: let all the inhabitants of the land tremble: for the day of the LORD cometh, for it is nigh at hand; ²**A day of darkness and of gloominess, a day of clouds and of thick darkness,** as the morning spread upon the mountains: a great people and a strong; there hath*

not been ever the like, neither shall be any more after it, even to the years of many generations." . . .

Verse 1:

"¹Blow ye the trumpet in Zion, and sound an alarm in my holy mountain: let all the inhabitants of the land tremble: for the day of the LORD cometh, for it is nigh at hand;

> ❖ **"let ALL inhabitants of the earth tremble." Would this include the FALSE PROPHET?**

Verse 2:

"²A day of darkness and of gloominess, a day of clouds and of thick darkness, as the morning spread upon the mountains: a great people and a strong; there hath not been ever the like, neither shall be any more after it, even to the years of many generations."

> ❖ **There's that Sun/Moon thing again!**

Joel 2:31-32:

"³¹The sun shall be turned into darkness, and the moon into blood, before the great and the terrible day of the LORD come.

³²And it shall come to pass, that whosoever shall call on the name of the LORD shall be delivered: for in mount Zion and in Jerusalem shall be deliverance, as the LORD hath said, and in the remnant whom the LORD shall call."

Verse 31:

*"³¹The sun shall be turned into darkness, and the moon into blood, **before** the great and the terrible day of the LORD come.*

> ❖ **Joel says that the COSMIC EVENTS will take place BEFORE the DAY of the LORD! According to Matthew 24, the COSMIC EVENTS take place AFTER the Great Tribulation has ended, and yet Joel tells us that people are still being saved----and the Wrath of God has not yet come.**

Verse 32:

*"³²And it shall come to pass, that **whosoever shall call on the name of the LORD shall be delivered**: for in mount Zion and in Jerusalem shall be deliverance, as the LORD hath said, and in the remnant whom the LORD shall call."*

❖ **What? People can still be saved? How is this possible? Those pre-tribulation folks said the Holy Spirit was taken out of the earth Before the opening of the seven years of tribulation! How can one be saved if the Holy Spirit is not still working in the earth?**

Joel 3:14-15

*"¹⁴Multitudes, multitudes in the valley of decision: for the day of the LORD is near in the valley of decision. ¹⁵**The sun and the moon shall be darkened, and the stars shall withdraw their shining.**"*

❖ **Cosmic events [Matthew.24, Luke 21, Revelation 6 under the sixth seal]**

Verse 14:

"¹⁴Multitudes, multitudes in the valley of decision: for the day of the LORD is near in the valley of decision.

❖ **This is the last call to salvation. It is after the Great Tribulation, but prior to the Day of the Lord.**

Amos 5:18-20

*"¹⁸Woe unto you that desire the day of the LORD! to what end is it for you? **the day of the LORD is darkness, and not light.** ¹⁹As if a man did flee from a lion, and a bear met him; or went into the house, and leaned his hand on the wall, and a serpent bit him. ²⁰**Shall not the day of the LORD be darkness, and not light? even very dark, and no brightness in it?**"*

❖ **Sun and moon, again?**

Matthew 24:28-30

"28For wheresoever the carcass is, there will the eagles be gathered together.

29Immediately after the tribulation of those days shall the sun be darkened, and the moon shall not give her light, and the stars shall fall from heaven, and the powers of the heavens shall be shaken:

30And then shall appear the sign of the Son of man in heaven: *and then shall all the tribes of the earth mourn, and they shall see the Son of man coming in the clouds of heaven with power and great glory."*

How much evidence does one need to understand that the DAY of the LORD is NOT tantamount to "seven years of tribulation". Jesus tells us that the COSMIC EVENTS prophesied in the Old Testament, take place AFTER the Great Tribulation is concluded. Joel tells us that these same COSMIC EVENTS precede the DAY of the LORD. It is this "DAY of the LORD" that Christ will rescue his Church from----and NOT seven years of tribulation.

Verse 29:

"29Immediately after the tribulation of those days shall the sun be darkened, and the moon shall not give her light, and the stars shall fall from heaven, and the powers of the heavens shall be shaken: "

❖ **"AFTER the tribulation of those days"!**

Luke 21:25-26

*"25And there shall be **signs in the sun, and in the moon, and in the stars**; and upon the earth distress of nations, with perplexity; the sea and the waves roaring;*

26Men's hearts failing them for fear, and for looking after those things which are coming on the earth: **for the powers of heaven shall be shaken."**

II Peter 3:10-12

*"¹⁰But the day of the Lord will come as a thief in the night; **in the which the heavens shall pass away with a great noise, and the elements shall melt with fervent heat, the earth also and the works that are therein shall be burned up.**

¹¹Seeing then that all these things shall be dissolved, what manner of persons ought ye to be in all holy conversation and godliness,

¹²**Looking for and hasting unto the coming of the day of God,** wherein the heavens being on fire shall be dissolved, and the elements shall melt with fervent heat?"*

Peter says we are "LOOKING FOR" the coming of the DAY OF GOD wherein "the elements will melt with fervent heat". If we are "looking for" this event, how can the rapture occur prior to that time when the "elements will melt with fervent heat?

Verse 10:

*"¹⁰**But the day of the Lord will come as a thief in the night;** in the which **the heavens shall pass away with a great noise, and the elements shall melt with fervent hea**t, the earth also and the works that are therein shall be burned up."*

❖ How does one fit a seven year "peace covenant" into this verse?

Verse 12:

*"¹²**Looking for and hasting unto** the coming of the **day of God,** wherein the heavens being on fire shall be dissolved, **and the elements shall melt with fervent heat?"***

Revelation 6:12-17

*"¹²And I beheld when he had opened the sixth seal, and, lo, there was a great earthquake; **and the sun became black as sackcloth of hair, and the moon became as blood;***

¹³*And the stars of heaven fell unto the earth, even as a fig tree casteth her untimely figs, when she is shaken of a mighty wind.*

¹⁴*And the heaven departed as a scroll when it is rolled together; and every mountain and island were moved out of their places.*

¹⁵*And the kings of the earth, and the great men, and the rich men, and the chief captains, and the mighty men, and every bondman, and every free man, hid themselves in the dens and in the rocks of the mountains;*

¹⁶*And said to the mountains and rocks, Fall on us, **and hide us from the face of him that sitteth on the throne, and from the wrath of the Lamb:***

¹⁷***For the great day of his wrath is come; and who shall be able to stand?"***

- ❖ **This is clearly the WRATH OF GOD----"for the great day of HIS WRATH has come", and it comes AFTER the great COSMIC EVENTS which follow the Great Tribulation.**

	Hiding From Wrath	The Lord Will Judge	Man Is Humbled	Destruction Of Sinners	**Cosmic Events**	Shake The Earth	Abolish Idols
Isaiah	2:10; 2:19; 2:21	2:11; 2:17; 13:6	2:11; 2:17; 13:7; 13:11	13:9; 13:11	**13:10; 13:13**	2:19; 13:13	2:18
Joel					**2:1-2; 2:10; 2:31; 3:15**	2:10; 3:16	
Amos					**5:18; 5:20**		
Zephaniah			1:14	1:17	**1:15**		1:18
Acts					**2:20**		
I Thess.				5:2-3			
II Peter		3:10					
Matthew					**24:29;**		
Revelation	6:15	6:17	6:15		**6:12**	6:14	

❖ The column identified in this grid as "cosmic events", clearly reflect the words of Jesus who said "immediately *AFTER the tribulation of those days,* the sun shall be darkened and the moon shall not give her light and the powers of the heavens shall be shaken, and THEN the sign of the coming of the Son of Man". Joel clearly tells us that these COSMIC EVENTS precede the coming DAY OF THE LORD. It is in this short period of time between the Cosmic Events and the DAY of the LORD that contains the "valley of decision"----man's last chance for salvation. What a merciful God we serve. It is THIS "day of the Lord" that we will be rescued from and NOT from "seven years of tribulation". It is the DAY of GOD wherein the elements shall melt with fervent heat.

Same day escape

II Peter 2:4-9

"⁴For if God spared not the angels that sinned, but cast them down to hell, and delivered them into chains of darkness, to be reserved unto judgment;

⁵And spared not the old world, but saved Noah the eighth person, a preacher of righteousness, bringing in the flood upon the world of the ungodly;

⁶And turning the cities of Sodom and Gomorrah into ashes condemned them with an overthrow, making them an ensample unto those that after should live ungodly;

⁷And delivered just Lot, vexed with the filthy conversation of the wicked:

⁸(For that righteous man dwelling among them, in seeing and hearing, vexed his righteous soul from day to day with their unlawful deeds;)

*⁹The Lord knoweth how to deliver the godly out of temptations, **and to reserve the unjust unto the day of judgment to be punished:"***

❖ **Anybody LEFT BEHIND here?**

Luke 17:28-30

"28Likewise also as it was in the days of Lot; they did eat, they drank, they bought, they sold, they planted, they builded;

29But **the same day that Lot went out of Sodom it rained fire and brimstone** *from heaven, and destroyed them all.*

*30***Even thus shall it be in the day when the Son of man is revealed."**

Verse 29:

"29But **the same day** *that Lot went out of Sodom it rained fire and brimstone from heaven,* **and destroyed them all.** *"*

❖ **SAME DAY!**

Verse 30:

"30Even thus shall it be **in the day when the Son of man is revealed."**

❖ **EVEN THUS - SAME DAY!**

When God shut the door of the ARK, it began to rain on the SAME DAY. When Lot was safely removed from Sodom, fire fell from heaven on the SAME DAY and destroyed them all! No one was "left behind" for seven years. Jesus said----"as it was in the days of Noah and Lot, so it will be in the coming of the son of man". It is difficult to understand how pre-tribulationists so utterly miss the mark on this very important point of "the Day of the Lord". Four issues are at hand here:

1. The pre-tribulationists declaration that the Day of the Lord begins with the opening of 7 years of tribulation simply cannot be validated in scripture. There is absolutely NOTHING to support this notion. It seems then, that pre-tribulationists go to great lengths to avoid any discussion of "tribulation" upon the church of the Latter Times.

"Escaping tribulation" should never be a litmus for the establishment of sound eschatology. There is no plum line or level in the pre-trib method of interpreting God's word. Long excepted standards of study, and development of doctrine, are totally abandoned regarding the identification of the Day of the Lord.

2. It is not "DISCOMFORT" that the Lord promises exemption from. It is not even "TRIBULATION" that the Lord promises deliverance from. It is only the Day of the Lord and HIS WRATH that the church will be exempt of. Tribulation is nothing new for the elect. The elect have always suffered persecution in some location and in every century throughout church history. To suggest that Tribulation, and the Wrath of God, are synonymous is ludicrous. Is every severe persecution that has assailed the church throughout the ages to be considered "The Wrath of God"? Early church leaders, and followers of Jesus, believed that the Day of the Lord was at hand BECAUSE OF tribulation. They were well aware of the fact that the "GREAT TRIBULATION" must occur FIRST, before their gathering by the Lord. They held that Anti-Christ must first appear [II Thessalonians 2] and that he will set up the Abomination of Desolation which would be the Flash Point to begin the Great Tribulation! They BELIEVED their Lord and the Apostles.

3. Neither God nor angles can dissuade the pre-tribulationist. God has said, "immediately AFTER the tribulation of those days, the sun and moon shall be darkened, the powers of the heavens shaken, and THEN the sign of the Son of Man in heaven --- He shall send His ANGELS to gather his elect "at that time [Matthew 24]. An ANGEL said (to John) "These are those who came out of GREAT TRIBULATION." I must

point out that these who "came out of Great Tribulation";
Revelation.7;14-------

    a.   were from every race on earth;

    b.   numbered in the multiplied millions;

    c.   they are the souls of the martyrs of the Great Tribulation

    d.   their bodies await the FIRST RESURECTION

Rev 7:13-14

13 And one of the elders answered, saying unto me, What are these which are arrayed in white robes? and whence came they?

*14 And I said unto him, Sir, thou knowest. And he said to me, **These are they which came out of great tribulation**, and have washed their robes, and made them white in the blood of the Lamb. KJV*

    5.   Pre-tribulationists simply FAIL to disclose any scripture supporting a "silent rapture". Every reference to their "Rapture" is based circumstantially, in many cases on conjecture, and in some cases on unadulterated FRAUD.

It must be understood that "the valley of decision" precedes the Day of the Lord. This will be mankind's LAST CHANCE for deliverance, and that day will come when the sun and moon are darkened and the powers of the heaven are shaken. There will be NO excuse in that day. Those appointed unto God's Wrath will be the only ones LEFT BEHIND! They will be destroyed "the same day" as the elect are gathered----so says Jesus.

1--- 3 1/2 years of great tribulation---the great martyrdom of Rev.20:4-6

2----great cosmic events----the Valley of Decision

3---the rapture----the Day of the Lord

Is the "tribulation" synonymous with the "GREAT AND TERRIBLE DAY OF THE LORD"?------ IMPOSSIBLE!!!

TEREO EK -------- *used 32 times in the New Testament*

Because the KJV Bible uses the words "KEPT FROM "in Revelation. 3;10, it appears to suggest [in the mind of the pre-tribulationist] that the Church will be KEPT FROM the Great Tribulation [wrath of God] via the Pre Tribulation Rapture. In fact, the original language suggests quite the opposite. The term "kept from" is actually interpreted from the Greek words TEREO EK. Let's take a close look at TEREO EK.

<u>Revelation.3;8-10</u>

*8 I know thy works: behold, I have set before thee an open door, and no man can shut it: for thou hast a little strength, **and hast kept my word**, and hast not denied my name.*

9 Behold, I will make them of the synagogue of Satan, which say they are Jews, and are not, but do lie; behold, I will make them to come and worship before thy feet, and to know that I have loved thee.

*10 **Because thou hast kept the word of my patience**, I also will **keep thee** from the hour of temptation, which shall come upon all the world, to try them that dwell upon the earth.*

A Bust on Tereo Ek

Because thou hast kept the word of my patience, I also will keep thee from [TEREO EK] the hour of temptation, which shall come upon all the world, to try them that dwell upon the earth.

keep/kept from

KJV - hold fast, keep (-er), (pre-, re-) serve, watch. NT:5083

tereo (tay-reh'-o); from teros (a watch; perhaps akin to NT:2334); to guard (from loss or injury, properly, by keeping the eye upon; and thus differing from NT:5442, which is properly to prevent escaping; and from NT:2892, which implies a fortress or full military lines of apparatus), i.e. to note (a prophecy; figuratively, to fulfil a command); by implication, to detain (in custody; figuratively, to maintain); by extension, to withhold (for personal ends; figuratively, to keep unmarried); by extension, to withhold (for personal ends; figuratively, to keep unmarried):

John 8:51-56

*51 Verily, verily, I say unto you, If a man **keep my saying**, he shall never see death.*

*52 Then said the Jews unto him, Now we know that thou hast a devil. Abraham is dead, and the prophets; and thou sayest, If a man **keep my saying**, he shall never taste of death.*

53 Art thou greater than our father Abraham, which is dead? and the prophets are dead: whom makest thou thyself?

54 Jesus answered, If I honour myself, my honour is nothing: it is my Father that honoureth me; of whom ye say, that he is your God:

*55 Yet ye have not known him; but I know him: and if I should say, I know him not, I shall be a liar like unto you: but I know him, **and keep his saying**.*

John 17:11-16

*11 And now I am no more in the world, but these are in the world, and I come to thee. Holy Father, **keep through** thine own name those whom thou hast given me, that they may be one, as we are.*

*12 While I was with them in the world, I kept them in thy name: those that thou gavest me **I have kept**, and none of them is lost, but the son of perdition; that the scripture might be fulfilled.*

13 And now come I to thee; and these things I speak in the world, that they might have my joy fulfilled in themselves.

14 I have given them thy word; and the world hath hated them, because they are not of the world, even as I am not of the world.

*15 I pray **NOT** that thou shouldest take them out of the world, but that thou shouldest **KEEP THEM FROM [tereo ek]** the evil.*

Cross reference to Revelation 3:10

2 Corinthians 11:9-11

*9 And when I was present with you, and wanted, I was chargeable to no man: for that which was lacking to me the brethren which came from Macedonia supplied: and in all things I have **kept myself** from being burdensome unto you, and so will I keep myself.*

10 As the truth of Christ is in me, no man shall stop me of this boasting in the regions of Achaia. KJV

Eph 4:2-3

2 With all lowliness and meekness, with longsuffering, forbearing one another in love;

*3 Endeavoring to **keep the unity** of the Spirit in the bond of peace. KJV*

1 Tim 5:22

*22 Lay hands suddenly on no man, neither be partaker of other men's sins: **keep thyself pure.** KJV*

1 Tim 6:14-15

*14 That thou **keep this commandment** without spot, unrebukeable, **until the appearing of our Lord Jesus Christ:***

James 1:27-2:1

*27 Pure religion and undefiled before God and the Father is this, To visit the fatherless and widows in their affliction, and to **keep himself unspotted from the world.** KJV*

James 2:10-11

*10 For whosoever shall **keep the whole law**, and yet offend in one point, he is guilty of all. KJV*

1 John 2:3-4

*3 And hereby we do know that we know him, **if we keep his commandments.** KJV*

1 John 3:22-23

*22 And whatsoever we ask, we receive of him, **because we keep his commandments**, and do those things that are pleasing in his sight. KJV*

1 John 5:2-6

*2 By this we know that we love the children of God, when we love God, **and keep his commandments.***

*3 For this is the love of God, **that we keep his commandments**: and his commandments are not grievous.*

*4 For whatsoever is born of God **overcometh the world**: and this is the victory that overcometh the world, even our faith.*

*5 **Who is he that overcometh the world**, but he that believeth that Jesus is the Son of God? KJV*

1 John 5:21

*21 Little children, **keep yourselves from idols**. Amen. KJV*

Jude 21-25

*21 **Keep yourselves in the love of God**, looking for the mercy of our Lord Jesus Christ unto eternal life.*

22 And of some have compassion, making a difference:

23 And others save with fear, pulling them out of the fire; hating even the garment spotted by the flesh.

*24 Now unto him that is **able to keep you from falling**, and to present you faultless before the presence of his glory with exceeding joy, **KJV***

Revelation 1:3-4

*3 Blessed is he that readeth, and they that hear the words of this prophecy, **and keep those things which are written therein: for the time is at hand.** KJV*

Revelation 12:17-13:1

17 And the dragon was wroth with the woman, and went to make war with the remnant of her seed, **which keep the commandments of God***, and have the testimony of Jesus Christ. KJV*

Revelation 14:12-13

12 Here is the patience of the saints: here are they that **keep the commandments of God,** *and the faith of Jesus. KJV*

Revelation 22:9-10

9 Then saith he unto me, See thou do it not: for I am thy fellowservant, and of thy brethren the prophets, and of **them which keep the sayings of this book***: worship God. KJV*

Revelation 3:8-11

8 I know thy works: behold, I have set before thee an open door, and no man can shut it: for thou hast a little strength, **and hast kept my word***, and hast not denied my name.*

9 Behold, I will make them of the synagogue of Satan, which say they are Jews, and are not, but do lie; behold, I will make them to come and worship before thy feet, and to know that I have loved thee.

10 **Because thou hast kept the word of my patience, I also will keep thee** *from the hour of temptation, which shall come upon all the world, to try them that dwell upon the earth. KJV*

Dear reader, I have shown EVERY verse in the New Testament using the Greek term TEREO or the combination TEREO EK. In EVERY CASE----it is the same. Tereo Ek means to "keep in, through, against, guard over, maintain, persevere to". It NEVER means "ESCAPE FROM"-----NEVER! God will keep [tereo EK] his Church in the Great Tribulation for "they overcame by the Blood of the Lamb and the word of their testimony and loved not their own lives even unto death" [Revelation. 12].

The RESTRAINER of II Thessalonians 2

2 Thess 2:6-7

6 And now ye know what withholdeth that he might be revealed in his time.

*7 For the mystery of iniquity doth already work: **only he who now letteth will let, until he be taken out of the way.** KJV*

It is held in Pre-Trib theology, that the "restraining force" of this verse is none other than the Holy Spirit indwelling the Church, and that the "Church" is that restraining force that keeps Antichrist from being revealed until that moment when the Church will be raptured and the Holy Spirit is removed from the earth. As I have said before, there is nothing in scripture to support such an allegation. It is based purely on conjecture. As a matter of fact, there IS such a RESTRAINER recorded in scripture. The Biblical standard for establishing a TRUTH is that the truth be established in the testimony of TWO WITNESSES. Those two witnesses are soundly established in the books of Daniel and Revelation and exactly in context to this matter.

OT:5975---CEASE

`amad (aw-mad'); a primitive root; to stand, in various relations (literal and figurative, intransitive and transitive):

KJV - abide (behind), appoint, arise, cease, confirm, continue, dwell, be employed, endure, establish, leave, make, ordain, be [over], place, (be) present (self), raise up, remain, repair, + serve, set (forth, over, -tle, up), (make to, make to be at a, with-) stand (by, fast, firm, still, up), (be at a) stay (up), tarry.

Dan 12:1-8

*12:1 And at that time shall Michael **stand up [AMAD----CEASE]**, the great prince which standeth for the children of thy people: **and there shall be a time of trouble, such as never was since there was a nation even to that same time**: and at that time thy people shall be delivered, every one that shall be found written in the book.*

*2 **And many of them that sleep in the dust of the earth shall awake,** some to everlasting life, and some to shame and everlasting contempt.*

3 And they that be wise shall shine as the brightness of the firmament; and they that turn many to righteousness as the stars forever and ever.

*4 But thou, O Daniel, shut up the words, and seal the book, **even to the time of the end**: many shall run to and fro, and knowledge shall be increased.*

5 Then I Daniel looked, and, behold, there stood other two, the one on this side of the bank of the river, and the other on that side of the bank of the river.

6 And one said to the man clothed in linen, which was upon the waters of the river, How long shall it be to the end of these wonders?

*7 And I heard the man clothed in linen, which was upon the waters of the river, when he held up his right hand and his left hand unto heaven, and sware by him that liveth forever **that it shall be for a time, times, and an half; and when he shall have accomplished to scatter the power of the holy people, all these things shall be finished. KJV***

There are four very important points to this portion of scripture-----

1   When the arch-angel Michael stands [Amad---ceases]--- the Great Tribulation begins

2   It will happen in the TIME OF THE END

3   The Great Tribulation will be three and one half years long

4   Antichrist will "scatter the power of the Holy People", and then the Tribulation will end.

Revelation 12:7-12

7 And there was war in heaven: **Michael and his angels fought against the dragon;** *and the dragon fought and his angels,*

8 And prevailed not; neither was their place found any more in heaven.

9 **And the great dragon was cast out, that old serpent, called the Devil, and Satan,** *which deceiveth the whole world:* **he was cast out into the earth, and his angels were cast out with him.**

10 And I heard a loud voice saying in heaven, Now is come salvation, and strength, and the kingdom of our God, and the power of his Christ: for the accuser of our brethren is cast down, which accused them before our God day and night.

11 **And they overcame him by the blood of the Lamb, and by the word of their testimony; and they loved not their lives unto the death.**

12 Therefore rejoice, ye heavens, and ye that dwell in them. **Woe to the inhabiters of the earth and of the sea! for the devil is come down unto you, having great wrath,** *because he knoweth that he hath but a short time. KJV*

There are four points to consider in this New testament passage

1   There is war in heaven---Michael does battle with Satan and his forces

2   Satan is cast out

3   The Saints overcome

4   Satan brings GREAT WRATH into the earth

These are the two witnesses to the identity of the "RESTRAINER" of II Thessalonians chapter two. It is undeniable. A war in the heavenlies has raged for millennia. That war has been fought between Satan and Michael [the arch angel protector over the children of Jacob]. In the time of the end, Satan and his angelic hoards will be cast into the earth. Through the agent of Antichrist, they will persecute the Jewish people and the Church for three and one half years. They bring GREAT WRATH to the earth. The Great Tribulation is NOT the "wrath of God". It is the "wrath of Satan". There are NO OTHER SCRIPTURES than these to identify the "RESTRAINER of II Thessalonians 2".

MY FRIEND DAVE

In my mind, Dave Mac Pherson is the greatest Post-tribulation eschatologist in the world today. He terrorizes those who teach pre-tribulationism---he terrorizes them with SCRIPTURE. He terrorizes them with recorded Church history. They fear him because they hate the truth. He exposes their foul doctrine and the history of pre-tribulationism going all the way back to 1830. He traces its growth in America and documents its proponents from Margaret Mac Donald [1830] to Tim Lahaye [Left Behind books]. Here is a very notable piece that has circled the earth. I would never teach Bible Prophecy without this paper.

Famous Rapture Watchers
By Dave MacPherson

"The following quotes - to which a couple more have been added - were first circulated in a little-known, non-copyrighted paper of mine in the 1970's. While noting how Revelation. 3:10 has been interpreted by the greatest Greek experts, can you determine the rapture view of each of the leaders herein?

Barnabas (40-100): "The final stumbling-block (or source of danger) approaches . . . for the whole [past] time of your faith will profit you nothing, unless now in this wicked time we also withstand coming sources of danger . . . That the Black One [Antichrist] may find no means of entrance . . ." (Epistle of Barnabas, 4).

Clement of Rome (40-100): " . . . the Scripture also bears witness, saying, 'Speedily will He come, and will not tarry'; and, 'The Lord shall suddenly come [Matthew 24:30 coming] to His temple, even the Holy One, for whom ye look'" (I Clement, 23).

Hermas (40-140): "Those, therefore, who continue steadfast, and are put through the fire [of the Great Tribulation that is yet to come], will be purified by means of it . . . Wherefore cease not speaking these things into the ears of the saints . . ." (The Pastor of Hermas, Vision 4).

Polycarp (70-167): "He comes as the Judge of the living and the dead" (Epistle to the Philippians, II).

Justin Martyr (100-168): "The man of apostasy [Antichrist], who speaks strange things against the Most High, shall venture to do unlawful deeds on the earth against us the Christians . . ." (Dialogue With Trypho, 110).

Melito (100-170): "For with all his strength did the adversary assail us, even then giving a foretaste of his activity among us [during the Great Tribulation] which is to be without restraint . . ." (Discourse on the Resurrection, i, 8).

Irenaeus (140-202): "And they [the ten kings who shall arise] shall lay Babylon waste, and burn her with fire, and shall give their kingdom to the beast, and put the church to flight" (Against Heresies, V, 26).

Tertullian (150-220): "The souls of the martyrs are taught to wait [Revelation. 6] . . . that the beast Antichrist with his false prophet may wage war on the Church of God . . ." (On the Resurrection of the Flesh, 25).

Hippolytus (160-240): " . . . the one thousand two hundred and three score days (the half of the week) during which the tyrant is to reign and persecute the Church, which flees from city to city, and seeks concealment in the wilderness among the mountains" (Treatise on Christ and Antichrist, 61).

Cyprian (200-258): "The day of affliction has begun to hang over our heads, and the end of the world and the time of the Antichrist to draw near, so that we must all stand prepared for the battle . . ." (Epistle, 55, 1).

Victorinus (240-303): " . . . the times of Antichrist, when all shall be injured" (Commentary on the Apocalypse of the Blessed John, VI, 5).

Lactantius (240-330): "And power will be given him [Antichrist] to desolate the whole earth for forty-two months . . . When these things shall so happen, then the righteous and the followers of truth shall separate themselves from the wicked, and flee into solitudes" (Divine Institutes, VII, 17).

Athanasius (293-373): " . . . they have not spared Thy servants, but are preparing the way for Antichrist" (History of the Arians, VIII, 79).

Ephraim the Syrian (306-373): "Nothing remains then, except that the coming of our enemy, Antichrist, appear . . ." (Sermo Asceticus, I).

Pseudo-Ephraem (4th century?): " . . . there is not other which remains, except the advent of the wicked one [Antichrist] . . ." (On the Last Times, the Antichrist etc., 2).

Cyril of Jerusalem (315-386): "The Church declares to thee the things concerning Antichrist before they arrive . . . it is well that, knowing these things, thou shouldest make thyself ready beforehand" (Catechetical Lectures, 15, 9).

Jerome (340-420): "I told you that Christ would not come unless Antichrist had come before" (Epistle 21).

Chrysostom (345-407): " . . . the time of Antichrist . . . will be a sign of the coming of Christ . . ." (Homilies on First Thessalonians, 9).

Augustine (354-430): "But he who reads this passage [Daniel 12], even half asleep, cannot fail to see that the kingdom of Antichrist shall fiercely, though for a short time, assail the Church . . ." (The City of God, XX, 23).

Venerable Bede (673-735): "[The Church's triumph will] follow the reign of Antichrist" (The Explanation of the Apocalypse, II, 8).

Bernard of Clairvaux (1090-1153): "There remains only one thing----that the demon of noonday [Antichrist] should appear, to seduce those who remain still in Christ . . ." (Sermons on the Song of Songs, 33, 16).

Roger Bacon (1214-1274): " . . . because of future perils [for the Church] in the times of Antichrist . . ." (Opus Majus, II, p. 634).

John Wycliffe (1320-1384): "Wherefore let us pray to God that he keep us in the hour of temptation, which is coming upon all the world, Revelation. iii" (Writings of the Reverend and Learned John Wickliff, D.D., p. 155).

Martin Luther (1483-1546): "[The book of Revelation] is intended as a Revelation of things that are to happen in the future, and especially of tribulations and disasters for the Church . . ." (Works of Martin Luther, VI, p. 481).

William Tyndale (1492-1536): " . . . antichrist preacheth not Peter's doctrine (which is Christ's gospel) . . . he compelleth all men with violence of sword" (Greenslade's The Work of William Tindale, p. 127).

Menno Simons (1496-1561): " . . . He will appear as a triumphant prince and a victorious king to bring judgment. Then will those who persecute us look upon Him . . ." (Complete Writings . . . , p. 622).

John Calvin (1509-1564): " . . . we ought to follow in our inquiries after Antichrist, especially where such pride proceeds to a public desolation of the church" (Institutes, Vol. 2, p. 411).

John Knox (1515-1572): " . . . the great love of God towards his Church, whom he pleased to forewarn of dangers to come, so many years before they come to pass . . . to wit, The man of sin, The Antichrist, The Whore of Babylon" (The History of the Reformation . . . , I, p. 76).

John Fox (1516-1587): " . . . that second beast prophesied to come in the later time of the Church . . . to disturb the whole Church of Christ . . ." (Acts and Monuments, I).

Roger Williams (1603-1683): "Antichrist . . . hath his prisons, to keep Christ Jesus and his members fast . . ." (The Bloody Tenent, of Persecution, p. 153).

John Bunyan (1628-1688): "He comes in flaming fire [as Judge] and . . . the trump of God sounds in the air, the dead to hear his voice . . ." (The Last Four Things: Of Judgment).

Daniel Whitby (1638-1726): " . . . after the Fall of Antichrist, there shall be such a glorious State of the Church . . . so shall this be the Church of Martyrs, and of those who had not received the Mark of the Beast . . ." (A Paraphrase and Commentary, p. 696).**

Increase Mather (1639-1723): "That part of the world [Europe] was to be principally the Seat of the Church of Christ during the Reign of Antichrist" (Ichabod, p. 64).

Matthew Henry (1662-1714): "Those who keep the gospel in a time of peace shall be kept by Christ in an hour of temptation [Revelation 3:10]" (Commentary, VI, p. 1134).

Cotton Mather (1663-1728): " . . . that New Jerusalem, whereto the Church is to be advanced, when the Mystical Babylon shall be fallen" (The Wonders of the Invisible World, p. 3).

Jonathan Edwards (1703-1758): " . . . continuance of Antichrist's reign [when the Church is persecuted] did not commence before the year of Christ 479 . . ." (A History of the Work of Redemption, p. 217).

John Wesley (1703-1791): "'The stars shall . . . fall from heaven,' (Revelation, vi. 13) . . . And then shall be heard the universal shout . . . followed by the 'voice of the archangel,' . . . 'and the trumpet of God' . . . (I Thessalonians iv. 16)." (The Works of the Revelation. John Wesley, A.M., Vol. V, p. 173).

George Whitefield (1714-1770): "... 'while the bridegroom tarried,' in the space of time which passeth between our Lord's ascension and his coming again to judgment ..." (Gillies' Memoirs of Revelation. George Whitefield, p. 471).

David Brainerd (1718-1747): "... and I could not but hope, that the time was at hand, when Babylon the great would fall and rise no more" (Memoirs ..., p. 326).

Morgan Edwards (1722-1795): "[Antichrist] has hitherto assumed no higher title than 'the vicar general of Christ on earth' ..." (Two Academical Exercises etc., p. 20).

John Newton (1725-1807): "'Fear not temptation's fiery day, for I will be thy strength and stay. Thou hast my promise, hold it fast, the trying hour [Revelation 3:10] will soon be past'" (The Works of the Revelation. John Newton, Vol. II, p. 152).

Adam Clarke (1762-1832): "We which are alive, and remain ... he [Paul] is speaking of the genuine Christians which shall be found on earth when Christ comes to judgment" (Commentary, Vol. VI, p. 550).

Charles G. Finney (1792-1875): "Christ represents it as impossible to deceive the elect. Matthew. 24:24. We have seen that the elect unto salvation includes all true Christians." (Lectures on Systematic Theology, p. 606).

Charles Hodge (1797-1878): "... the fate of his Church here on earth ... is the burden of the Apocalypse" (Systematic Theology, Vol. III, p. 827).

Albert Barnes (1798-1870): "... he will keep them in the future trials that shall come upon the world [Revelation 3:10]" (Notes on the New Testament, p. 94).

George Mueller (1805-1898): "The Scripture declares plainly that the Lord Jesus will not come until the Apostasy shall have taken place, and the man of sin ... shall have been revealed ..." (Mrs. Mueller's Missionary Tours and Labours, p. 148).

Benjamin W. Newton (1805-1898): "The Secret Rapture was bad enough, but this [John Darby's equally novel idea that the book of Matthew is on 'Jewish' ground instead of 'Church' ground] was worse" (unpublished Fry MS. and F. Roy Coad's Prophetic Developments, p. 29).

R. C. Trench (1807-1886): " . . . the Philadelphian church . . . to be kept in temptation, not to be exempted from temptation . . ." (Seven Churches of Asia, pp. 183-184).

Carl F. Keil (1807-1888): " . . . the persecution of the last enemy Antichrist against the church of the Lord . . ." (Biblical Commentary, Vol. XXXIV, p. 503).

Henry Alford (1810-1871): "Christ is on His way to this earth [I Thessalonians 4:17] . . ." (The New Testament for English Readers, Vol. II, p. 491).

John Lillie (1812-1867): "In his [Antichrist's] days was to be the great----the last----tribulation of the Church" (Second Thessalonians, pp. 537-538).

F. L. Godet (1812-1900): "The gathering of the elect [Matthew 24:31] . . . is mentioned by St. Paul, 1 Thess. 4:16, 17, 2 Thess. 2:1 . . ." (Commentary on Luke, p. 452).

Robert Murray McCheyne (1813-1842): "Christians must have 'great tribulation'; but they come out of it" (Bonar's Memoirs of McCheyne, p. 26).

S. P. Tregelles (1813-1875): "The Scripture teaches the Church to wait for the manifestation of Christ. The secret theory bids us to expect a coming before any such manifestation" (The Hope of Christ's Second Coming, p. 71).

Franz Delitzsch (1813-1890): " . . . the approaching day is the day of Christ, who comes . . . for final judgment" (Commentary on Hebrews, Vol. II, p. 183).

C. J. Ellicott (1819-1905): "[I Thessalonians 4:17] 'to meet the Lord,' as He is coming down to earth . . ." (Commentary on the Thessalonian Epistles, p. 66).

Nathaniel West (1826-1906): "[The Pre-Trib Rapture] is built on a postulate, vicious in logic, violent in exegesis, contrary to experience, repudiated by the early Church, contradicted by the testimony of eighteen hundred years . . . and condemned by all the standard scholars of every age" (The Apostle Paul and the "Any Moment" Theory, p. 30).

Alexander Maclaren (1826-1910): "He will keep us in the midst of, and also from, the hour of temptation [Revelation 3:10]" (The Epistles of John, Jude and the Book of Revelation, p. 266).

J. H. Thayer (1828-1901): "To keep [Revelation 3:10]: . . . by guarding, to cause one to escape in safety out of" (A Greek-English Lexicon of the New Testament, p. 622).

Adolph Saphir (1831-1891): " . . . the advent of the Messiah . . . to which both the believing synagogue and the church of the Lord Jesus Christ are looking . . ." (The Epistle to the Hebrews, Vol. I, p. 96).

M. R. Vincent (1834-1922): "The preposition ['from'] implies, not a keeping from temptation, but a keeping in temptation [Revelation 3:10] . . ." (Word Studies . . . , p. 466).

William J. Erdman (1834-1923): " . . . by the 'saints' seen as future by Daniel and by John are meant 'the Church' . . ." (Notes on the Book of Revelation, p. 47).

H. Grattan Guinness (1835-1910): " . . . the Church is on earth during the action of the Apocalypse . . ." (The Approaching End of the Age, p. 136).

H. B. Swete (1835-1917): "The promise [of Revelation 3:10], as Bede says, is 'not indeed of your being immune from adversity, but of not being overcome by it'" (The Apocalypse of St. John, p. 56).

William G. Moorehead (1836-1914): "... the last days of the Church's deepest humiliation when Antichrist is practicing and prospering (Dan. viii:12) ..." (Outline Studies in the New Testament, p. 123).

A. H. Strong (1836-1921): "The final coming of Christ is referred to in: Mat. 24:30 ... [and] I Thess. 4:16 ..." (Systematic Theology, p. 567).

Theodor Zahn (1838-1933): "... He will preserve ... at the time of the great temptation [Revelation 3:10] ..." (Zahn-Kommentar, I, p. 305).

I. T. Beckwith (1843-1936): "The Philadelphians ... are promised that they shall be carried in safety through the great trial [Revelation 3:10], they shall not fall" (The Apocalypse of John, p. 484).

Comings which is an absurdity" (Scriptural Truth About the Lord's Return, p. 16). Robert Cameron (1845-1922): "The Coming for, and the Coming with, the saints, still persists, although it involves a manifest contradiction, viz., two Second

B. B. Warfield (1851-1921): "... He shall come again to judgment ... to close the dispensation of grace ..." (Biblical Doctrines, p. 639).

David Baron (1855-1926): "(Tit. ii. 13), for then the hope as regards the church, and Israel, and the world, will be fully realised" (Visions of Zechariah, p. 323).

Philip Mauro (1859-1952): "... 'dispensational teaching' is modernistic in the strictest sense ... it first came into existence within the memory of persons now living ..." (The Gospel of the Kingdom, p. 8).

A. T. Robertson (1863-1934): "In Revelation. 3:10 ... we seem to have the picture of general temptation with the preservation of the saints" (A Grammar of the Greek New Testament in the Light of Historical Research, p. 596).

R. C. H. Lenski (1864-1936): " . . . it [Philadelphia] shall be kept untouched and unharmed by the impending dangers [Revelation 3:10]" (The Interpretation of St. John's Revelation, pp. 146-146).

William E. Biederwolf (1867-1939): "Godet, like most pre-millennial expositors, makes no provision for any period between the Lord's coming for His saints and His coming with them . . ." (The Second Coming Bible, p. 385).

Alexander Reese (1881-1969): " . . . we quite deliberately reject the dispensational theories, propounded first about 1830 . . ." (The Approaching Advent of Christ, p. 293).

Norman S. MacPherson (1899-1980): " . . . the view that the Church will not pass into or through the Great Tribulation is based largely upon arbitrary interpretations of obscure passages" (Triumph Through Tribulation, p. 5)."

Isn't it amazing? Such an uproar over a doctrine that has no history. Millions of books sold to support a complete MYTH----and sold by those who profess to be agents of TRUTH. Isn't it revealing that there is not ONE MENTION of a pre-tribulation rapture in all the thousands of extant Church documents in the world today. Don't you think that there would be SOMETHING? Aren't you curious to know why there is this great SILENCE pre dating the year 1830. Think of all the great Church expositors throughout the ages----and NOT ONE will support your belief that there will be a resurrection of the righteous prior to the Great Tribulation.

Revelation 20:4-6

4 I saw thrones on which were seated those who had been given authority to judge. And I saw the souls of those who had been beheaded because of their testimony for Jesus and because of the word of God. They had not worshiped the beast or his image and had not received his mark on their foreheads or their hands. They came to life and reigned with Christ a thousand years.

5(The rest of the dead did not come to life until the thousand years were ended.) This is the first resurrection.

6 Blessed and holy are those who have part in the first resurrection. The second death has no power over them, but they will be priests of God and of Christ and will reign with him for a thousand years.

Pre-tribulationism is a GIANT in terms of "numbers". It is the dominant position in pre-millenial eschatology today------and yet it all comes to NOTHING with FIVE LITTLE WORDS----*"This is the first resurrection".*

Such nonsense surrounds this pre-trib fallacy-----a "silent rapture-----all the little children will be raptured without their parents----the perpetual antichrist----multiple trumpets separated in time", on and on and on, and all in a desperate attempt to excuse that which is inexcusable. Allow these great men of "famous rapture watchers" to speak to you. Many of these notables were martyred in the Church age. They can be found in the New Testament----

Revelation 6:9-11

*9 And when he had opened the fifth seal, I saw under the altar **the souls of them that were slain for the word of God, and for the testimony which they held:***

*10 And they cried with a loud voice, saying, **How long, O Lord**, holy and true, dost thou not judge and avenge our blood on them that dwell on the earth?*

*11 And white robes were given unto every one of them; and it was said unto them, that they should rest yet for a little season, **until their fellow servants also and their brethren, that should be killed as they were, should be fulfilled.** KJV*

HOW LONG? How long indeed? How long until the Church awakens from its delusion? How long till the pre-trib DOPE wears off and the Church is left with a three and one half year HANGOVER? Your denial will not make it all go away. It will HAPPEN, not because I say it will happen, but because the BIBLE says it will happen. "Say it's not so----say it's not so" cry the pew sheep. "Tell me something to make it all go away" is the plea. It won't go away! The Church is called to ENDURE the Great Tribulation!

The Church today is marching locked-step toward many horrifying events. The destruction of Babylon will cause the current economic situation to look like economic paradise, and we are not even concerned about WHO Babylon really is, even though Revelation 18:4 commands us to flee from her. The New Testament tells us several times that Babylon is "THAT GREAT CITY"------WHAT GREAT CITY? Don't you think it is important to find out? Following the destruction of Babylon, Antichrist will rise and Great tribulation will follow----

Revelation 14:6-12

❖ *6 Then I saw another angel flying in midair, **and he had the eternal gospel to proclaim to those who live on the earth- to every nation**, tribe, language and people.*

The Gospel is being freely preached in the earth

❖ *7 He said in a loud voice, "Fear God and give him glory, because the hour of his judgment has come. Worship him who made the heavens, the earth, the sea and the springs of water."*

❖ *8 A second angel followed and said, "Fallen! Fallen is Babylon the Great, which made all the nations drink the maddening wine of her adulteries."*

Babylon falls

❖ *9 A third angel followed them and said in a loud voice: "If anyone worships the beast and his image and receives his mark on the forehead or on the hand, 10 he, too, will drink of the wine of God's fury, which has been poured full strength into the cup of his wrath. He will be tormented with burning sulfur in the presence of the holy angels and of the Lamb. 11 And the smoke of their torment rises forever and ever. There is no rest day or night for those who worship the*

> beast and his image, or for anyone who receives the mark of his name." NIV

The Beast rises to power

❖ *Rev 17:16-18:1*

*16 And the ten horns which thou sawest upon the beast, these shall hate the whore, **and shall make her desolate and naked, and shall eat her flesh, and burn her with fire.***

Babylon is destroyed

❖ *17 For God hath put in their hearts to fulfil his will, and to agree, **and give their kingdom unto the beast, until the words of God shall be fulfilled.***

The Beast rises to power

❖ *18 And **the woman which thou sawest is that great city,** which reigneth over the kings of the earth. KJV*

That GREAT CITY

SEVEN YEARS of TRIBULATION?

It is broadly taught in evangelical circles, that there will be SEVEN YEARS of tribulation following the rapture. It is further taught that Antichrist will rise after the chaos of the missing millions of Raptured Christians. One of his first tasks at hand will be to establish a seven year PEACE COVENANT between Israel and her Arab neighbors. He will make provision through this alleged treaty, to re-build the Temple of God that was destroyed in 70 AD. This is believed to be accomplished in the first three and one half years of the seven year reign of Antichrist. In the middle of the alleged seven years, antichrist will betray the Jews and set up an image of himself in the temple, thus desecrating the temple and triggering the GREAT TRIBULATION. It is taught that this "time of distress" is divided into TWO time components----the tribulation [first 3 1/2 years], and the GREAT TRIBULATION [remaining 3 1/2 years]. This, they claim, to be supported by Daniel 9:27---"and he shall confirm the covenant with many for one week, and in the midst of the week he [antichrist] shall cause the sacrifice and oblations to cease". It is vital to know that this scripture reference is the centerpiece of the notion that there will be seven years of tribulation.

CHAPTER II

The SEVENTY WEEKS of Daniel

OT:7657shib` iym. (shib-eem'); multiple of OT:7651; seventy: KJV - seventy, threescore and ten (+-teen).OT:7620shabuwa` (shaw-boo'-ah); or shabua` (shaw-boo'-ah); also (feminine) shebu`ah (sheb-oo-aw'); properly, passive participle of OT:7650 as a denominative of OT:7651; literal, sevened, i.e. a week (specifically, of years): KJV - seven, week.

Dan 9:24

24 ***Seventy weeks [shabiym shabuwa]*** *are determined upon thy people and upon thy holy city, to finish the transgression, and to make an end of sins, and to make reconciliation for iniquity, and to bring in everlasting righteousness, and to seal up the vision and prophecy, and to anoint the most Holy.*

SHIBIYM SHABUA------Seventy Weeks are determined on ISRAEL

PURPOSE:

1. finish the transgression

2. to make and end of sins

3. to make reconciliation for iniquity-------Isaiah 53

4. to bring in everlasting righteousness

5. to seal up the vision and prophecy

6. to anoint the Most Holy

*25 Know therefore and understand, that from the going forth of the commandment to restore and to build Jerusalem **unto the Messiah** the Prince shall be **seven weeks and threescore and two weeks:** the street shall be built again, and the wall, even in troublous times.*

SEVEN/SHEBA----------SEVENS/SHABUAH [Seven Weeks of years] = 49 years to restore and rebuild Jerusalem.

OT:7651

sheba` (sheh'-bah); or (masculine) shib` ah (shib-aw'); from OT:7650; a primitive cardinal number; seven (as the sacred full one); also (adverbially) seven times; by implication, a week; by extension, an indefinite number:

KJV - (+by) seven [-folds],-, [-teen, -teenth], -th, times). Compare OT:7658.

*26 **And after threescore and two weeks** shall Messiah be cut off, but not for himself: and the people of the prince that shall come shall destroy the city and the sanctuary; and the end thereof shall be with a flood, and unto the end of the war desolations are determined.*

-SIXTY TWO SHABUAHS [weeks of years] following the SEVEN WEEKS of years [for rebuilding] = 49 + 434 years = 483 years TO THE COMING OF MESSIAH-------and AFTER the SIXTY and TWO WEEKS [49 years +434 years] shall Messiah be cut off [in the midst of the 70th week]-------seven weeks/49 years for rebuilding + sixty two weeks/434 years to Messiah + one half week---3 1/2 years to the CROSS = sixty nine and one half weeks/489.5 years from the declaration of Artaxerxes in 458 B.C. to the CROSS! There is one half week [three and one half years] remaining in the seventy weeks of Daniel. Desolations are determined unto the END! That is when the remaining three and one half years will conclude the "seventy weeks of Daniel".

*"The PEOPLE of the prince that shall come **shall destroy the city and the sanctuary;"** Daniel 9;27*

- ❖ The people who destroyed the sanctuary [temple] were the Syrian wing of the ROMAN ARMY, and their PRINCE was TITUS-------70AD. Pre-tribulationist attempt to separate the "people of the prince that shall come"----- from that prince himself, by saying that there is a 2,000 year GAP between the two. They agree that the "people of the prince" was the Roman Army that destroyed the TEMPLE in 70AD, but go on to contend that the PRINCE THAT IS TO COME is none other than a future [un-named] "antichrist" to appear some two thousand years later.

*27 And he shall confirm **the covenant** with many for one week: **and in the midst of the week he shall cause the sacrifice and the oblation to cease,** and for the overspreading of abominations he shall make it desolate, even until the consummation, and that determined shall be poured upon the desolate.*

- ❖ Note carefully that the verse states "the covenant" rather than "a covenant". This is very critical to know, for the "covenant" spoken of in this passage speaks of an already existing covenant----and not of a FUTURE PEACE AGREEMENT posed by Antichrist.

the covenant
briyth (ber-eeth')
a compact [made by passing between pieces of flesh] -- confederacy, (con-)feder(-ate), covenant, league.

- ❖ This "covenant" [briyth] is an OLD TESTAMENT tradition of establishing a binding agreement made by severing the carcass of an animal with the participants passing between the severed halves. It simply CANNOT BE that the "covenant [briyth]" of Daniel 9;27 could be initiated by a Roman [gentile] prince two thousand five hundred years into the future since this "briyth" is a uniquely HEBREW tradition and would NEVER be used in an agreement

between Israel and her Arab [gentile] neighbors-----
NEVER!

❖ *"And HE shall CONFIRM the **covenant** with many for ONE
WEEK [one SEVEN/SHEBUA]"*

❖ "HE", being a PERSONAL PRONOUN, can only be assigned
to the most recent PERSONAL PROPER NOUN of the
passage. That most recent PERSONAL PROPER NOUN is---
----"MESSIAH". This linguistic rule is so in English, Hebrew
and Greek. Verse 25 holds the most recent Personal
PROPER NOUN of the passage. That personal proper
noun is "MESSIAH". It is emphatically "MESSIAH" who will
confirm THE covenant with the many, and in the midst of
the SEVEN [week], he shall cause the sacrifice and oblation
to cease.

In the "MIDST OF THE WEEK", HE [Messiah] shall cause the
sacrifice and oblation to cease. Three and one half years into
Christ's ministry [in the midst of the 70th week of Daniel], he
cried out----"IT IS FINISHED". He caused the animal sacrifice for
sin to CEASE!

458 B.C.----from the going forth of the decree to restore and
rebuild----"

In 458 B.C., the Persian King Artaxerxes decreed that the Jews
should "restore and rebuild Jerusalem". It is noteworthy that this
starting date [458 BC] places the appearing of the promised Savior
and King of the Jews at 26 AD. The Gospel of Luke makes it very
clear that Jesus was baptized by John and publicly proclaimed to
be the promised Messiah in the "fifteenth year of the reign of
Tiberius Caesar" (Luke 3:1). Tiberius Caesar began his rule in 11
A.D. Therefore the fifteenth year of Tiberius would be 26 A.D. This
historical fact brings us to the mathematical conclusion of exactly
sixty nine weeks [483 years] from the decree of Artaxerxes [458
BC] to the baptism of Jesus in 26 AD -----sixty nine weeks of years
to Messiah. Only the Seventieth week [7 years] remains from that

point. Jesus therefore entered the SEVENTIETH WEEK OF DANIEL at his baptism in 26 AD. If you do the math in this account, don't forget that there is no ZERO YEAR between 1 BC and 1 AD. It is ONE YEAR between 1 BC and 1 AD, causing this account to be mathematically perfect.

John 2:18-21

18 Then the Jews demanded of him, "What miraculous sign can you show us to prove your authority to do all this?"

19 Jesus answered them, "Destroy this temple, and I will raise it again in three days."

20 The Jews replied, "It has taken forty-six years to build this temple, and you are going to raise it in three days?"

21 But the temple he had spoken of was his body. NIV

In a desperate attempt to retain their notion of a future "seven years of tribulation", modern "theologians" will contend that Augustus Caesar died in 14/15 AD and that Tiberius came to power at the passing of Augustus thereby invalidating the claim that the "seventieth week [the baptism of Jesus]" commenced in 26 A.D. noting that according to Luke "John came baptizing in the 15th year of the reign of Tiberius"----adding 15 years to the official regency of Tiberius following the death of Augustus in 15 A.D. would bring the baptism of Jesus to 30 A.D. which would serve to DISMISS the decree of Artaxerxes in 458 B.C. from consideration as the starting point of the seventy weeks prophecy. It is true that Augustus did die in 14 A.D but Tiberius assumed the role of "co-regent" to Augustus in 11 A.D. This is a historical fact. This is obviously the starting point of Luke's account of the baptism of Jesus "in the fifteenth year of the reign of Tiberius" as we shall discover.

Modern theologians would point to a much earlier decree by Cyrus the Great------[Ezra 1:1-4] decreed in 536 B.C.----- adding the sixty nine weeks [483 years] "unto Messiah" to that date would bring that reckoning to 53 B.C as the conclusion of the sixty ninth week, some decades before Christ was even born. Another "decree" that is used to invalidate the 26 A.D. anointing of Jesus is that decree of Darius in 520 B.C. [Ezra 4:24]. That decree would bring the end of the 69 weeks of years [483 years] to 37 B.C , also much too soon to be prophetically significant. It is only the decree of Artaxerxes in 458 B.C. that brings sanity to the "Seventy Weeks of Daniel".

Add to this, the declaration of John 2;20 and we unravel this question with the authority of God's Word. Historians tell us with great certainty that the Eighteenth year of King Herod's reign was 18/19 B.C. That is when the renewal project for the Second Temple began. Adding the "forty six years" of John 2: 20 brings us to exactly 27A.D. [considering that there is no ZERO YEAR to count]. 27 A.D. was clearly the year following the baptism of Jesus, that this proclamation of John 2:20 was made. That proclamation of John 2;20 serves to invalidate any claims that Jesus was baptized and began his ministry in any other year than 26 A.D.---exactly sixty nine weeks of years following the decree of Artaxerxes in 458 B.C. and forty five years following the commencement of the rebuilding of the second temple. This cannot be denied. Jesus opened the SEVENTIETH WEEK of DANIEL at his Baptism in 26 A.D, and in the midst of the Seventieth Week he caused the sacrifice for sin to CEASE [Passover 30 A.D.] thereby leaving us to identify the remaining three and one half years which contain "THE GREAT TRIBULATION" spoken by Daniel, Jesus, Paul, and John the Revelator.

This therefore, clearly dates the baptism of Christ and His anointing by the Holy Spirit at the same time as the fulfillment of Daniel's prophecy "unto Messiah". It also places Christ's death on the Cross at 30 A.D., the very time when Daniel prophesied that the Messiah would be "cut off, but not for himself".

It is important to know that the crucifixion of Jesus took place precisely in the MIDST OF THE [seventieth] WEEK----also prophesied in Daniel 9----verse 27. These facts are beyond question. It is not possible that such a prophecy could be so precise unless it was supernatural. It could not possibly be "circumstantial". It is

Christ who fulfilled the COVENANT MADE WITH ABRAHAM, that in his SEED all the nations of the earth would be blessed. It is the ABRAHAMIC COVENANT that was "confirmed" in 30 A.D., causing the sacrifices for SIN to CEASE!

"he shall confirm the covenant with many"

OT:1285----"covenant"

beriyth (ber-eeth'); from OT:1262 (in the sense of cutting [like OT:1254]); a compact (because made by passing between pieces of flesh): -confederacy, [con-] feder [-ate], covenant, league.

OT:2677----"in the midst of the week"

chetsiy (khay-tsee'); from OT:2673; the half or middle:

KJV - half, middle, mid [-night], midst, part, two parts.

"And for the OVERSPREADING OF ABOMINATIONS---------"

OT:8251-----"abominations"

shiqquwts (shik-koots'); or shiqquts (shik-koots'); from OT:8262; disgusting, i.e. filthy; especially idolatrous or (concretely) an idol:

KJV - *abominable filth* (idol, -ation), detestable (thing).

'he shall make it desolate------"

OT:8074----desolate

shamem (shaw-mame'); a primitive root; to stun (or intransitively, grow numb), i.e. *devastate* or (figuratively) stupefy (both usually in a passive sense):

KJV - make amazed, be astonied, (be an) astonish (-ment), (be, bring into, unto, lay, lie, make) *desolate* (-ion, places), be destitute, destroy (self), *(lay, lie, make) waste*, wonder.

"even unto the CONSUMMATION-------"

OT:3617----"consumation"

kalah (kaw-law'); from OT:3615; *a completion*; adverb, completely; also *destruction*:

KJV - altogether, (be, utterly) consume (-d), consummation (-ption), was determined, *(full, utter) end, riddance.*

"and that determined shall be poured upon the DESOLATE".

Matt 24:1-2

24:1 And Jesus went out, and departed from the temple: and his disciples came to him for to shew him the buildings of the temple.

2 And Jesus said unto them, See ye not all these things? verily I say unto you, There shall not be left here one stone upon another, that shall not be thrown down.

3. and Jerusalem shall be trodden down of the gentiles till the times of the gentiles has been fulfilled.

Over 1900 years have passed since this prophesy of Jesus was fulfilled in 70 AD. Such desolation as to cause Samuel Clemmons [Mark Twain] to remark----"this is the most desolate place on earth", as he visited Palestine on his famous world tour in the early 1900s. It was only from 1948 that the land began to bloom again, signaling the approach to the end of the TIMES of the Gentiles.

So folks, you see, this entire premise of SEVEN YEARS of TRIBULATION is based on the corrupt interpretation of Daniel 9:27. The ONLY references to "tribulation" in the Bible presents a time frame of three and one half years. The first half of the 70th week of Daniel was fulfilled in the ministry of Christ, and desolations were determined unto the end----------THEN the remaining three and one half years of the Seventieth Week of Daniel will be fulfilled in the event of the reign of Antichrist and GREAT TRIBULATION.

Matt 24:15-22

*15 When ye therefore shall see the abomination of desolation, spoken of by Daniel the prophet, **stand in the holy place**, (whoso readeth, let him understand:)*

16 Then let them which be in Judaea flee into the mountains:

17 Let him which is on the housetop not come down to take anything out of his house:

18 Neither let him which is in the field return back to take his clothes.

19 And woe unto them that are with child, and to them that give suck in those days!

20 But pray ye that your flight be not in the winter, neither on the Sabbath day:

21 For then shall be great tribulation, such as was not since the beginning of the world to this time, no, nor ever shall be.

*22 And except those days should be shortened, there should no flesh be saved: **but for the elect's sake those days shall be shortened.** KJV*

Please note that there is NO MENTION of "seven years" in the entire Olivette Discourse. The disciples asked Jesus to show them the signs of the end. In all of this, there is never mentioned "seven years", and only that the time of Great Tribulation would be triggered by the Abomination spoken of by the prophet Daniel. As a matter of fact, there is no mention of SEVEN YEARS anywhere in the New testament------NOT ONCE! If this notion of "seven years" of tribulation was to be a part of our understanding of New Testament eschatology, don't you think that "seven years" might be found in the Olivette Discourse or certainly in the book of

Revelation? The fact is-----it is not to be found ANYWHERE in the Bible [outside of the erroneous interpretation of Daniel 9:27].

2 Thess 2:1-4

*2:1 Now we beseech you, brethren, **by the coming of our Lord Jesus Christ, and by our gathering together unto him,***

*2 That ye be not soon shaken in mind, or be troubled, neither by spirit, nor by word, nor by letter as from us, **as that the day of Christ is at hand.***

*3 Let no man deceive you by any means: **for that day shall not come,** except there come a falling away first, **and that man of sin be revealed**, the son of perdition;*

*4 Who opposeth and exalteth himself above all that is called God, or that is worshipped; so that **he as God sitteth in the temple of God, shewing himself that he is God.***

The Apostle Paul reiterates in this brief passage, that the DAY OF OUR GATHERING will NOT COME until there is a great apostasy and ANTICHRIST IS REVEALED. This event will trigger the great tribulation just as Jesus has said. Jesus and Paul have the very same thing to say about this event. It is that same event prophesied in the book of Daniel chapter 12.

The Biblical TIME of Tribulation

Dan 12:6-7

*6 And one said to the man clothed in linen, which was upon the waters of the river, **How long shall it be to the end of these wonders?***

*7 And I heard the man clothed in linen, which was upon the waters of the river, when he held up his right hand and his left hand unto heaven, and sware by him that liveth for ever **that it shall be for a time, times, and an half; and when he shall have accomplished to scatter the power of the holy people, all these things shall be finished.** KJV*

Rev 12:13-14

13 And when the dragon saw that he was cast unto the earth, he persecuted the woman which brought forth the man child.

*14 And to the woman were given two wings of a great eagle, that she might fly into the wilderness, into her place, **where she is nourished for a time, and times, and half a time, from the face of the serpent.** KJV*

Rev 13:4-5

4 And they worshipped the dragon which gave power unto the beast: and they worshipped the beast, saying, Who is like unto the beast? who is able to make war with him?

*5 And there was given unto him a mouth speaking great things and blasphemies; **and power was given unto him to continue forty and two months.** KJV*

I was a pre-tribulationist for over twenty five years. There were always problems for me in this belief. Mathew 24 was a nightmare. It seemed to clearly point to a post-tribulation Rapture. All of the Gospel references to the "HARVEST of souls" clearly pointed to the END of the AGE. II Thessalonians 2 [Paul] tells us that it is impossible for the Rapture to come before Antichrist abominates the Temple. There is not even a Temple to abominate. It was destroyed in 70 AD, long after Paul's martyrdom. So it must be that a THIRD TEMPLE will be built. When we see that Temple being built, then we can observe, as the signs of Jesus Return rapidly fall into place.

Then there were all those scriptures encouraging us to "*look for* the coming of the Lord---wherein the elements would melt with fervent heat". This did not sound like anything I had been taught. There was all those verses in the Gospels that spoke of ANGELS gathering the HARVEST at the END OF THE AGE. I avoided the book of Revelation like a deadly plague. It was a hodge podge of confusion for me. I was more astute than most Christians regarding this topic, and yet the more I studied the matter, the more confused I became.

The average Christian never takes the time to actually study the matter. Most, simply believe what they have been told from the pulpit or in "Bible Study". As a matter of fact, you might be labeled a "trouble maker" if you attempt to get straight answers from those who teach the Doctrine of Imminence and the Pre-Tribulation Rapture. This writing is in NO WAY an exhaustive study in the TRUTH about the Rapture. As a matter of fact, it only skirts the edges of what is certainly a very broad and lengthy subject. If we are indeed living in the latter times----then I suggest that you step up to your mirror and look deeply into the eyes of the person you see in that mirror and say "HELLO----TRIBULATION SAINT".

Babylon MUST FALL

Brace yourselves folks----there will be no RAPTURE/ RESURRECTION before BABYLON FALLS. The book of Revelation clearly reveals this to anyone who will simply sit down and read it.

1 The gospel will be preached in all the earth

2 Babylon will fall

3 The empire of the BEAST will rise

Rev 14:6-10

*6 And I saw another angel fly in the midst of heaven, **having the everlasting gospel to preach unto them that dwell on the earth, and to every nation**, and kindred, and tongue, and people,*

7 Saying with a loud voice, Fear God, and give glory to him; for the hour of his judgment is come: and worship him that made heaven, and earth, and the sea, and the fountains of waters.

*8 And there followed another angel, saying, **Babylon is fallen, is fallen, that great city,** because she made all nations drink of the wine of the wrath of her fornication.

*9 And the third angel followed them, saying with a loud voice, **If any man worship the beast and his image, and receive his mark in his forehead, or in his hand,**

10 The same shall drink of the wine of the wrath of God, which is poured out without mixture into the cup of his indignation; and he shall be tormented with fire and brimstone in the presence of the holy angels, and in the presence of the Lamb:

Rev 17:15-18:1

15 And he saith unto me, The waters which thou sawest, where the whore sitteth, are peoples, and multitudes, and nations, and tongues.

16 And the ten horns which thou sawest upon the beast, these shall hate the whore, **and shall make her desolate and naked, and shall eat her flesh, and burn her with fire.**

17 **For God hath put in their hearts to fulfil his will, and to agree, and give their kingdom unto the beast, until the words of God shall be fulfilled.**

18 And the woman which thou sawest **is that great city,** which reigneth over the kings of the earth.

WHO IS BABYLON THE GREAT [Revelation 18]?

- ❖ **Whoever she is-----she is "that great city"**

- ❖ **Whoever she is------she is the greatest IMPORT NATION the world has ever seen**

- ❖ **Whoever she is, she has DEEP WATER SEAPORTS**

- ❖ **Whoever she is------the merchants of the earth are going to grieve their losses**

- ❖ Whoever she is------she will be destroyed in ONE DAY

- ❖ Whoever she is-----she is the greatest nation that has ever existed on earth.

- ❖ Whoever she is-----God has come to hate her.

- ❖ Whoever she is------she will NEVER RISE AGAIN.

- ❖ Whoever she is------God has commanded----COME OUT OF HER MY PEOPLE

- ❖ Whoever she is-----she is the LAST of all the Great Nations [Jer. 50:12]

- ❖ Whoever she is---she was born of another great nation

- ❖ Whoever she is------her destruction will bring about the rise of Antichrist!

"and they [the ten kings that shall arise] shall lay Babylon waste, and burn her with fire, and shall give their kingdom to the Beast, AND PUT THE CHURCH TO FLIGHT" Irenaeus----disciple of Polycarp,-----disciple of John.

"and there was given unto him [the Beast] a mouth speaking great things, and blasphemies; and power was given unto him to continue **FORTY AND TWO MONTHS**; and he opened his mouth in blasphemy against God, to blaspheme his name, and his tabernacle [the Church], and them that dwell in heaven; **and it was given unto him to make WAR WITH THE SAINTS, and to overcome them**, and power was given him over all kindreds, and tongues, AND NATIONS, and all that dwell upon the earth shall worship him whose names are not written in the Book of Life of the Lamb slain from the foundation of the world" **Revelation 13:5-10.**

TAKE YOUR HEAD OUT OF THE SAND

THERE AIN'T NO RAPTURE TODAY, TOMORROW, NEXT WEEK, MONTH , YEAR!

It cannot be. The Great Tribulation will follow the destruction of Mystery Babylon. The rapture/resurrection will occur immediately AFTER the Tribulation of those days [Dan.12. Matt.24, Mark 13. Luke 21, Rev 20;4-7]. Your opinion of WHO Mystery Babylon is, does not matter regarding this study. You need only to know that MYSTERY BABYLON will fall before the GREAT TRIBULATION begins. The Bible calls us to ENDURE TO THE END!

HE THAT OVERCOMES--------and ENDURES TO THE END

NT:----"overcome"

nikao (nik-ah'-o); from NT:3529; to subdue (literally or figuratively):

KJV - conquer, overcome, prevail, get the victory.

<u>1 John 5:4-6</u>

*4 For whatsoever is born of God **overcometh the world**: and this is the victory that overcometh the world, even our faith.*

*5 Who is he that **overcometh** the world, but he that believeth that Jesus is the Son of God?*

<u>Rev 2:7-8</u>

*7 He that hath an ear, let him hear what the Spirit saith unto the churches; To him that **overcometh** will I give to eat of the tree of life, which is in the midst of the paradise of God.*

<u>Rev 2:11-12</u>

*11 He that hath an ear, let him hear what the Spirit saith unto the churches; **He that overcometh shall not be hurt of the second death**.*

<u>Rev 2:17-18</u>

*17 He that hath an ear, let him hear what the Spirit saith unto the churches; To **him that overcometh** will I give to eat of the hidden manna, and will give him a white stone, and in the stone a new name written, which no man knoweth saving he that receiveth it.*

<u>Rev 2:26-27</u>

*26 And **he that overcometh, and keepeth my works unto the end**, to him will I give power over the nations:*

<u>Rev 3:5-6</u>

*5 **He that overcometh, the same shall be clothed in white raiment**; and I will not blot out his name out of the book of life, but I will confess his name before my Father, and before his angels. [White Raiment---**Rev 7:9-14 these are those that came out of GREAT TRIBULATION]***

<u>Rev 3:12-13</u>

*12 **Him that overcometh will I make a pillar in the temple of my God**, and he shall go no more out: and I will write upon him the name of my God, and the name of the city of my God, which is new Jerusalem, which cometh down out of heaven from my God: and I will write upon him my new name.*

<u>Rev 3:21-4:1</u>

*21 **To him that overcometh will I grant to sit with me in my throne**, even as I also overcame, and am set down with my Father in his throne.*

22 He that hath an ear, let him hear what the Spirit saith unto the churches.

<u>Rev 21:7-9</u>

*7 **He that overcometh shall inherit all things**; and I will be his God, and he shall be my son.*

8 But the fearful, and unbelieving, and the abominable, and murderers, and whoremongers, and sorcerers, and idolaters, and all liars, shall have their part in the lake which burneth with fire and brimstone: which is the second death.

HE THAT ENDURES

NT:5278----"endure"

hupomeno (hoop-om-en'-o); from NT:5259 and NT:3306; to stay under (behind), i.e. remain; figuratively, to undergo, i.e. bear (trials), have fortitude, persevere:

KJV - abide, endure, (take) patient (-ly), suffer, tarry behind.

Matt 10:22-23

22 And ye shall be hated of all men for my name's sake: **but he that endureth to the end shall be saved.**

Matt 24:13-15

13 **But he that shall endure unto the end, the same shall be saved.**

14 And this gospel of the kingdom shall be preached in all the world for a witness unto all nations; and then shall the end come.

Mark 13:13-14

13 And ye shall be hated of all men for my name's sake: **but he that shall endure unto the end, the same shall be saved.**

1 Thess 4:15-18

15 For this we say unto you by the word of the Lord, that we which are **alive and remain** *unto the coming of the Lord shall not prevent them which are asleep.*

*16 For the Lord himself shall descend from heaven with a shout, with the voice of the archangel, and with the **trump of God**: and the dead in Christ shall rise first:*

*17 Then we which are alive **and remain** shall be caught up together with them in the clouds, to meet the Lord in the air: and so shall we ever be with the Lord.*

18 Wherefore comfort one another with these words.

NT:4035-----"remain"

perileipo (per-ee-li'-po); from NT:4012 and NT:3007; to leave all around, i.e. (passively) survive: KJV - remain.

There are quite literally hundreds of scriptures that clearly dismiss the DOCTRINE OF IMMINENCE and place clear BIBLICAL PARAMETERS to the "COMING OF THE LORD". It will not happen today, next year, the year after that or the year after that. It will happen after the fall of Babylon----followed by the Great Tribulation and when that latest of Biblical signs comes to pass----- when the Sun and moon are darkened and the powers of the heavens are shaken------ THEN----the rapture will be imminent!

REVELATION 14 CHRONOLOGY

Verse 6] FIRST ANGEL---the *"EVER LASTING GOSPEL"* is preached in all the earth.

Verse 8] SECOND ANGEL------- *"Babylon is fallen, THE GREAT CITY"*

Verse 9] THIRD ANGEL---------the MARK OF THE BEAST

The chronology of these events leaves no room for doubt. The Gospel is being freely preached in the earth-------TO ALL. Babylon the Great FALLS, and the BEAST KINGDOM rises-------the MARK OF THE BEAST. It simply cannot be coincidental that THIS PASSAGE [Rev.14:6-10] mirrors EXACTLY the words of Irenaeus;

"and they [the ten kings that shall arise] shall lay Babylon waste, and burn her with fire, and shall give their kingdom to the Beast, AND PUT THE CHURCH TO FLIGHT" Irenaeus----disciple of Polycarp,-----disciple of John.

Can the views of modern eschatologists be regarded as SUPERIOR to that of the DIRECT CHURCH DECENDANT of JOHN? I think not.

Armageddon

ARMAGEDDON IS NOT AN EVENT! "ARMAGEDDON" is a LOCATION!

Revelation 16:16

"¹⁶And he gathered them together into a place called in the Hebrew tongue Armageddon."

LOCATION! LOCATION! LOCATION!

Movie portrayals of Armageddon have little to do with the real place and event. "Armageddon" is a long, broad valley in Israel (the Valley of Megiddo). Many of us have seen beautiful photos of this place. It is a beautiful, grassy valley eastward from Mount Carmel. There is room for literally millions of people standing shoulder to shoulder in this place. This is WHERE the great prophetic battle between Christ (with His Saints), against Satan (and his followers) will take place. It is emphatically NOT a place where the world comes to an abrupt end and ALL mankind is obliterated. Remember This, You heard it HERE, "HOLLYWOOD KNOWS NOTHING!" Repeat after me – "HOLLYWOOD KNOWS NOTHING ABOUT ARMAGEDDON".

The following is the Biblical scenario:

The nations of the earth will gather together at the end of the 42 months prophesied in the Bible. That 42 months will end with the gathering of the remainder of earth's military forces at the Valley of Megiddo, in Israel. With the death of the TWO WITNESSES who have resisted antichrist and his cohorts, these armies are arrayed for the final conflict of the ages. The winner takes all! But the outcome is unexpected-----------

The DAY OF THE LORD

Revelation 19:11-21

"¹¹And I saw heaven opened, and behold a white horse; and he that sat upon him was called Faithful and True, and in righteousness he doth judge and make war.

¹² His eyes were as a flame of fire, and on his head were many crowns; and he had a name written, that no man knew, but he himself.

¹³And he was clothed with a vesture dipped in blood: and his name is called The Word of God.

¹⁴And the armies, which were in heaven followed him upon white horses, clothed in fine linen, white and clean.

*¹⁵And out of his mouth goeth a sharp sword, **that with it he should smite the nations**: and he shall rule them with a rod of iron: and he treadeth the winepress of the fierceness and wrath of Almighty God.*

¹⁶And he hath on his vesture and on his thigh a name written, KING OF KINGS, AND LORD OF LORDS.

*¹⁷And I saw an angel standing in the sun; and he cried with a loud voice, saying to all the fowls that fly in the midst of heaven, **Come and gather yourselves together unto the supper of the great God;***

*¹⁸**That ye may eat the flesh of kings, and the flesh of captains, and the flesh of mighty men, and the flesh of horses, and of them that sit on them, and the flesh of all men, both free and bond, both small and great.***

¹⁹And I saw the beast, and the kings of the earth, and their armies, gathered together to make war against him that sat on the horse, and against his army.

²⁰And the beast was taken, and with him the false prophet that wrought miracles before him, with which he deceived them that had received the mark of the beast, and them that worshipped his image. These both were cast alive into a lake of fire burning with brimstone.

²¹And the remnant were slain with the sword of him that sat upon the horse, which sword proceeded out of his mouth: and all the fowls were filled with their flesh."

The outcome is settled. The mortality of earth's armies is 100%. Christ's losses, ZERO! What about Satan?

Revelation 20:2-3

"²And he laid hold on the dragon, that old serpent, which is the Devil, and Satan, and bound him a thousand years,

³And cast him into the bottomless pit, and shut him up, and set a seal upon him, that he should deceive the nations no more, till the thousand years should be fulfilled: and after that he must be loosed a little season."

❖ **Satan is bound for 1000 years, not to deceive the earth again till, the thousand years has expired. This is the millennial reign of Jesus.**

Revelation 20-6

*"⁶Blessed and holy is he that hath part in the first resurrection: on such the second death hath no power, **but they shall be priests of God and of Christ, and shall reign with him a thousand years.**"*

The Millennial Reign of Christ

<u>*Isaiah 2:1-4*</u>

"¹The word that Isaiah the son of Amoz saw concerning Judah and Jerusalem.

²And it shall come to pass in the last days, that the mountain of the LORD'S house shall be established in the top of the mountains, and shall be exalted above the hills; and all nations shall flow unto it.

³And many people shall go and say, Come ye, and let us go up to the mountain of the LORD, to the house of the God of Jacob; and he will teach us of his ways, and we will walk in his paths: for out of Zion shall go forth the law, and the word of the LORD from Jerusalem.

⁴And he shall judge among the nations, and shall rebuke many people: and they shall beat their swords into plowshares, and their spears into pruning hooks: nation shall not lift up sword against nation, neither shall they learn war anymore."

<u>*Micah 4:1-4*</u>

"¹But in the last days it shall come to pass, that the mountain of the house of the LORD shall be established in the top of the mountains, and it shall be exalted above the hills; and people shall flow unto it.

²And many nations shall come, and say, Come, and let us go up to the mountain of the LORD, and to the house of the God of Jacob; and he will teach us of his ways, and we will walk in his paths: for the law shall go forth of Zion, and the word of the LORD from Jerusalem.

³And he shall judge among many people, and rebuke strong nations afar off; and they shall beat their swords into plowshares, and their spears into pruning hooks: nation shall not lift up a sword against nation, neither shall they learn war any more.

⁴But they shall sit every man under his vine and under his fig tree; and none shall make them afraid: for the mouth of the LORD of hosts hath spoken it."

Revelation 20:4-6

"⁴And I saw thrones, and they sat upon them, and judgment was given unto them: and I saw the souls of them that were beheaded for the witness of Jesus, and for the word of God, and which had not worshipped the beast, neither his image, neither had received his mark upon their foreheads, or in their hands; and they lived and reigned with Christ a thousand years.

⁵But the rest of the dead lived not again until the thousand years were finished. **This is the first resurrection.**

⁶Blessed and holy is he that hath part in the first resurrection: on such the second death hath no power, but they shall be priests of God and of Christ, and shall reign with him a thousand years."

- ❖ **During this millennial reign, there will be literally millions of human beings born into the earth. These will be the offspring of the remnant of mankind that survived "THE DAY of THE LORD", which began soon after that day when the sun and moon were darkened (following the tribulation) and extending to the end of the 42 month (Timeline). Every man must be equally tempted in order to make an honest choice for following Jesus. These, who will be born during the millennium, have not been tempted as we, for Satan has been bound throughout their lives. How shall they receive eternal life in heaven? They must be tempted! They must be BORN AGAIN!**

Revelation 20:7-8

"⁷And when the thousand years are expired, Satan shall be loosed out of his prison,

⁸And shall go out to deceive the nations which are in the four quarters of the earth, Gog and Magog, to gather them together to battle: the number of whom is as the sand of the sea."

"... and all shall go out to deceive the nations."

- ❖ **What will be the outcome? Will some be deceived?**

Revelation 20:10

*"¹⁰And the devil that deceived them was cast into the lake of fire and brimstone, **where the beast and the false prophet are**, and shall be tormented day and night forever and ever."*

❖ "... and the devil that DECEIVED THEM" was cast into the Lake of fire where antichrist and the False prophet ARE (present tense). Antichrist (the beast) and the False Prophet have awaited their masters' arrival in Hell for one thousand years. Perhaps they believed that Satan could somehow prevail but – GUESS WHO's COMING FOR DINNER?

If you have questions about eternal judgment then read the following:

Revelation 20:10

*"¹⁰And the devil that deceived them was cast into the lake of fire and brimstone, **where the beast and the false prophet are**, and shall be tormented day and night forever and ever."*

❖ "... they shall be TORMENTED with fire FOREVER." Was antichrist (the beast) a real human being? Of course he was. Was the False Prophet a human being? Of course he was. Will humans suffer eternal torment? YOU ANSWER THE QUESTION!

A NEW HEAVEN AND EARTH

Revelation 21:1-6

"¹And I saw a new heaven and a new earth: for the first heaven and the first earth were passed away; and there was no more sea.

²And I John saw the holy city, new Jerusalem, coming down from God out of heaven, prepared as a bride adorned for her husband.

³And I heard a great voice out of heaven saying, Behold, the tabernacle of God is with men, and he will dwell with them, and they shall be his people, and God himself shall be with them, and be their God.

⁴And God shall wipe away all tears from their eyes; and there shall be no more death, neither sorrow, nor crying, neither shall there be any more pain: for the former things are passed away.

⁵And he that sat upon the throne said, Behold, I make all things new. And he said unto me, Write: for these words are true and faithful.

⁶And he said unto me, It is done. I am Alpha and Omega, the beginning and the end. I will give unto him that is athirst of the fountain of the water of life freely."

ETERNITY!!!!!----------------------------

CHAPTER III

A VERY MYSTERIOUS NATION

There is a mysterious nation alluded to in Isaiah 18. It is a nation that God will destroy prior to the judgment of the whole earth during the coming DAY OF THE LORD. To attain the identity of this nation, one must look closely at the original language [Hebrew]; To do otherwise will leave one to conclude that this "nation" is some obscure ancient people of North Central Africa, who can never be identified in the study of ancient Bible lands. This afore mentioned nation is prophetic, and holds great eschatological significance to the Church, and indeed to its people------and the WHOLE WORLD as we shall see.

"WOE TO THE NATION SHADOWING WITH WINGS"

TSELATSAL ---- OT 6767

"a REDUPLICATING SOUND------CLATTER OF WINGS"

"WHICH IS BEYOND THE RIVERS OF ETHIOPIA"

"RIVERS"

NAHAR---O.T. 5104

"STREAM or SEA"

"ETHIOPIA"

KUWSH---O.T.1573

NORTH AFRICA

"THAT SENDETH AMBASSADORS BY SEA"

"AMBASSADORS"

TSIYR----O.T. 6735

"A HINGE---PRESSED IN TURNING"

"MENTAL PRESSURE" as to intimidate

"BY SEA"

YAM---O.T.3220

"TO ROAR"

"A BREAKING SURF"

"TO THE WEST"

"EVEN IN VESSELS OF BULRUSHES UPON THE WATER"

"VESSELS"

KELIY---OT 3627

"APPARATUS"

"IMPLIMENT"

"VESSEL or WEAPON"

"ARMOUR"

"ARTILLERY"

"OF BULRUSHES"

GOME---OT 1572

"BULRUSH"

"SPECIFICALLY THE PAPYRUS"

"SAYING; GO YE SWIFT MESSENGER"

MAL'AK---OT 4397

"A DISPATCH"

"A MESSENGER OF GOD"

"AN ANGEL OR PROPHET"

"TO A PEOPLE TERRIBLE FROM THEIR BEGINNING HITHERTO"

"TERRIBLE"

YARE---OT3372

"TO FEAR"

"TO REVERE"

"TO CAUSE FRIGHT"

"HITHERTO"

HALEAH---OT 1973

"TO THE DISTANCE"

"FAR AWAY"

"ALSO IN TIME"

"BEYOND"

"FORTH"

"YONDER"

"TO A NATION METED OUT":

"METED OUT"

QAV-QAV---OT 6978

"FASTENED"

"STALWART"

"METED OUT"

"AND TRODDEN DOWN".

MEBUWCAH---OT 4001

"TRAMPLED"

"TREADED UNDER FOOT"

"WHOSE LAND THE RIVERS HAVE SPOILED""

"SPOILED"

BAZA---OT 958

"TO CLEAVE"

"ALL YE INHABITERS OF THE WORLD, AND DWELLERS ON THE EARTH, SEE YE, WHEN HE LIFTETH UP AN ENSIGN ON THE MOUNTAINS; AND WHEN HE BLOWETH A TRUMPET, HEAR YE"

"FOR SO THE LORD SAID UNTO ME, I WILL TAKE MY REST, AND I WILL CONSIDER IN MY DWELLING PLACE LIKE A CLEAR HEAT UPON HERBS, AND LIKE A CLOUD OF DEW IN THE HEAT OF HARVEST"

"FOR AFORE THE HARVEST"

"AFORE"PANIYM---OT 6440

"BEFORE"

"AGAINST"

"FOREFRONT"

"WHEN THE BUD IS PERFECT, AND THE SOUR GRAPE IS RIPENING IN THE FLOWER, HE SHALL BOTH CUT OFF THE SPRIGS WITH PRUNNING HOOKS, AND TAKE AWAY AND CUT DOWN THE BRANCHES"

"THEY SHALL BE LEFT TOGETHER UNTO THE FOULS OF THE MOUNTAINS, AND TO THE BEASTS OF THE EARTH: AND THE FOULS SHALL SUMMER UPON THEM, AND ALL THE BEASTS OF THE EARTH SHALL WINTER UPON THEM."

"IN THAT TIME SHALL THE PRESENT BE BROUGHT UNTO THE LORD OF HOSTS--------

- ❖ As in ancient days; the CAPTORS paraded their CONQUERED PEOPLES before the KING--------the destruction of THESE PEOPLE will satisfy the RIGHTEOUS JUDGMENT of the Lord of the Universe. They are a renowned people, and TALL IN STATURE. They are a people who are FIERCELY INDEPENDENT to the point of PRIDE and OBSTINANCE.

Danny McDowell

"OF A PEOPLE SCATTERED, AND PEELED"

"SCATTERED"

MASHAK---OT 4900

"SOW"

"SCATTER"

"STRETCH OUT"

"PEELED"

MOWRAT---OT 4178

"OBSTINATE"

"INDEPENDENT"

"AND FROM A PEOPLE TERRIBLE FROM THEIR BEGINNING HITHERTO; A NATION METED OUT AND TRODDEN UNDER FOOT, WHOSE LAND THE RIVERS HAVE SPOILED, TO THE PLACE OF THE NAME OF THE LORD OF HOSTS, THE MOUNT ZION".

- ❖ This "present" will be paraded before the Lord of Heaven and Earth as a witness to his righteous judgment.

- ❖ To those who would dismiss this explanation, I would ask these questions:

1. What is your explanation of those devices hovering above the nation in verse 1.?

2. Who would send "ambassadors by sea" to intimidate other nations [verse 2]?

3. Who would this people be that are spread abroad, obstinate, and fiercely independent?

4. What nation on earth has many interior borders, many of which are distinguished by the rivers that flow North to South, and East to West, and West to East over a continental divide.

5. What continent is WESTWARD beyond the crashing surf of West Africa?

Isa 17:1-2

17:1 The burden of Damascus. Behold, **Damascus is taken away from being a city, and it shall be a ruinous heap.** KJV

❖ Damascus has never been destroyed in human history. If that is so, then that "destruction" must be inherently a FUTURE EVENT. Who is this mystery nation whose destruction follows the destruction of Damascus described in the immediate preceding chapter of Isaiah? What is that characterization in time spoken of as "when the grape is beginning to ripen?" What is the connection to MYSTERY BABYLON of the book of Revelation?

1. In Revelation 14:6, we see that the Gospel is being freely preached in the earth.

2. In Revelation 14:8, we hear the declaration; "BABYLON IS FALLEN".

3. In Revelation 14:9 we hear the warning, "if any man worship the BEAST and his image, or receive his mark------------". These angelic declarations are CHRONOLOGICAL IN TIME.

❖ In Revelation 14:15, the declaration of the HARVEST OF THE EARTH--------"BECAUSE THE HARVEST OF THE EARTH IS RIPE"------and verse 18 declares "HER GRAPES ARE FULLY RIPE". *Do you see the pre-tribulation destruction of Babylon in this study? Do you understand that the GREAT TRIBULATION, and the DAY OF THE LORD will follow the destruction of Babylon/U.S.A.?*

1. The destruction of Damascus [Isaiah:17].

2. The destruction of that nation "shadowing with wings [Isaiah 18]"----Babylon of Revelation 14.----- when the" SOUR GRAPE IS RIPENING IN THE VINE".

3. And the GREAT TRIBULATION following the destruction of Babylon.

4. The "HARVEST OF THE EARTH WHEN THE GRAPE IS FULLY RIPE"----following the GREAT TRIBULATION

This is why it is so important to understand the URGENCY to obey the command to FLEE BABYLON as recorded in Revelation 18:4. A destruction will come to America that is recorded over and over in the writings of Isaiah, Jeremiah, and in the book of Revelation. The evidence would surely convince any jurist of sound reason. Time and again, the Lord warns us of what is to come and COMMANDS US TO FLEE!!

CHAPTER IV

DOMINIONISM

Dominioinism is not a late doctrine, although it has been altered over the centuries to adapt to contemporary prejudices. It's earliest record is associated with Catholicism. It was the teaching of the Roman Church, that the "CHURCH" would convert the entire world into a "one world Church/State", with the Pontiff being the Supreme Leader. It is in Church Dominion that Christ will rule the earth-----not in his bodily form, but in his surrogate-----the Church of Rome. This is the origin of Dominionism.

During the "Protestant Reformation" the Dominion Doctrine evolved into a Protestant Eschatology of course. The Pope became [in their doctrine] Antichrist persecuting the "true Church" [protestants], the great oppressions against protestants became the "GREAT TRIBULATION" and many other adjustments evolved in doctrine to satisfy the gross and well deserved antagonism against the Church of Rome.

Following the great separation between Rome and the protestant Churches, Dominionism developed further. The Pope remained the Antichrist system [in the eyes of reformers], and scriptures regarding the Great Tribulation were allegorized into current circumstantial events. It was the Reformed Church that declared that "one thousand years of Christ's rule in the earth" was never to be literal, but allegorical as the Catholics had previously taught, the difference being, the notable new adjunct to Christian influence-----now protestant.

Later in time, Dominionism developed into a hybrid mish mash of pre-millennialism, Dominionism, and Pre-tribulationism-----a ridiculous mixture that makes absolutely no sense whatsoever. A perfect example would be Pat Robertson's contention that we are living in the Last Days and the coming of Christ is imminent, but on the other hand, great revival will sweep across the world and earth's governments will be dominated by Christians. An oxymoron indeed-----or should I just say----"moron"? Many of today's evangelicals hold to this insane doctrine. Some of those being----

Fredrick Price

Leroy Jenkens

Creflo Dollar

Pat Robertson

A.A. Rutivi--Kenya

Robert Kayanja---Uganda

Nicholas Duncan-Williams----Ghana

David Oyepedo----Nigeria

Kenneth Copeland

Morris Cerrillo

Kenneth Hagin

Rick Joyner

C.P. Wagner

most of the TBN and Word of Faith ministries.

Please read these words carefully-------"ONLY THE PHYSICAL RETURN OF JESUS CHRIST WILL BRING RIGHTEOUSNESS INTO THE EARTH"! That event is not imminent, but it will happen soon. Jesus has clearly told us that "all flesh will perish" if he does not return to save the remnant of mankind from all the destructions that are coming on the earth. In fact, the apostle Paul absolutely refutes the notion that the Church will influence government in the earth. Paul tells us that there will be a great APOSTASIA [apostasy] prior to Christ's return [II Thess. 2]. The Church Universal will become more and more apostate, and MANY false Christ's ["anointed"] will arise and deceive MANY with wonderful works and miracles. In my second home of Uganda, there are Churches with the very name "Miracle Center"-----they are here----NOW-----coming in Christ's name--- and claiming to be "anointed".

John 14:1-3 *"Do not let your hearts be troubled. Trust in God; trust also in me. In my Father's house are many rooms; if it were not so, I would have told you. I am going there to prepare a place for you. And if I go and prepare a place for you,* **I will come back** *and take you to be with me that you also may be where I am."*

Matthew 26:64

"Yes, it is as you say," Jesus replied. "But I say to all of you: In the future you will see the **Son of Man** *sitting at the right hand of the Mighty One* **and coming on the clouds of heaven."**

Luke 21:27

At that time they will see the **Son of Man coming in a cloud with power and great glory.**.

Acts 1:11

"Men of Galilee," they said, "why do you stand here looking into the sky? This same Jesus, who has been taken from you into heaven, **will come back in the same way you have seen him go into heaven."**

Matthew 24:29-30

"Immediately after the distress of those days "`the sun will be darkened, and the moon will not give its light; the stars will fall from the sky, and the heavenly bodies will be shaken.' "At that time **the sign of the Son of Man will appear in the sky,** and all the nations of the earth will mourn.

Rev 1:7

Look, he is coming with the clouds, and **every eye will see him,** even those who pierced him; and all the peoples of the earth will mourn because of him. So shall it be! Amen.

Philippians 3:21

who, by the power that enables him to bring everything under his control, will transform our lowly bodies so that they will be like **his glorious body.**

Zechariah 14:3

Then the LORD will go out and fight against those nations, as he fights in the day of battle. On that day **his feet will stand on the Mount of Olives,** east of Jerusalem, and the **Mount of Olives will be split in two from east to west,** forming a great valley, with half of the mountain moving north and half moving south.

Titus 2:13

while we wait for the blessed hope-- **the glorious appearing** of our great God and Savior, Jesus Christ,

Matthew 24:30

They **will see the Son of Man coming** on the clouds of the sky, **with power and great glory.**

The notion that HUMAN FLESH [the Church] is capable of curing the world's problems is absurd. We are not called to solve the world's problems. We are called to be SEPERATE from the world and to adjoin ourselves to another Kingdom which is emphatically

NOT OF THIS WORLD. UTTER FAILURE has followed the efforts of the nations of Earth to find PERMANENT PEACE! Why would it be SANE to believe that a greedy, spiritually incestuous, doctrinally detoured, unlearned, and divided Church would be capable of bringing sanity into the whole earth-----and maintaining that sanity for one thousand years? I DON"T THINK SO!

UNDER THE MANGO TREE

There's a small village about twenty kilometers from Mbale Uganda. In that village lives a small number of God's people. They have no building in which to worship. They gather under a MANGO TREE. Images flood through my mind as I think about my precious siblings in Christ who gather in this way. This is truly the heart of a New Testament Church. It is the manifest expression of the words of Paul-----

Eph 2:19-22

19 Now therefore ye are no more strangers and foreigners, but fellow citizens with the saints, *and of the household of God*;

20 And are built upon the foundation of the apostles and prophets, *Jesus Christ himself being the chief corner stone;*

21 *In whom all the building fitly framed together groweth unto an holy temple in the Lord*:

22 *In whom ye also are builded together for an habitation of God through the Spirit.*

Can you imagine? Would you gather UNDER THE MANGO TREE, or do you require cushioned pews, air conditioning, and a grand display from your "music department". Would a couple of village drums suffice? I imagine in my mind----that God is leaning forward with great pride, and exclaiming----"NOW THAT'S MY CHURCH------- under that Mango Tree".

The day may come----when you also will gather----UNDER THE MANGO TREE.

The Church of Jesus Christ which meets UNDER THE MANGO TREE

Note the offering in the basket. The sum is less than three cents. Someone gave two empty match boxes. That's how poor these people are, but their gifts unto God are MAGNIFICENT! I might take this opportunity to say------"this may well be a demonstration of how the Church may survive in the days of Great Tribulation".

CHAPTER V

Abhorrent Traditions

Over the centuries the Church has picked up a lot of dirt, like a snowball rolling across a gravel pit. Many of our erroneous beliefs and traditions began shortly after the death of the Apostles. Those leaders who followed in the steps of the Apostles were faced with a constant and persistent attack from false teachers and heretics. The "push back" was valiant, but TIME and Satan were not cooperative. By the third century, there were so many corrupt teachings and customs that it was a stroll through the park for the Roman Emperor, Constantine the Great, to merge PAGANISM into Christianity, Church with State, and a complete transformation was well on its way. With rabid anti-Semitism saturating the Church, every semblance of our Jewish root was driven from our thought and practice.

Whereas the Lord's Table had previously been celebrated yearly in the DAYS OF UNLEAVENED BREAD, the Church turned the corner toward Romanized practices after the harsh treatment of those who persisted in orthodoxy. Nearly all succumbed to Roman pressure and the Lord's Table became institutionalize in "Holy communion". Power drifted upward and away from the local assembly to ROME. Christianity quickly transformed from a "faith" to a CULTURE, and remains so today. The Lord's Table at Passover was shoved aside and EASTER took its place. "CHRIST MASS" soon replaced the detailed account of Luke 1-2-and 3 regarding the birth of Christ----never mind that Luke held emphatically that no other teaching was known in all of the Churches than that which he revealed in his gospel [Luke 1].

BORN IN DECEMBER?

In the fourth century A.D. there existed tension and strife between the growing Church of Rome, and the religious factions of more ancient sources. Most of those ancient [pagan] religions can be traced all the way back to Babylon. In an effort to quell outbreaks of violence between the religious factions of Rome, Constantine [emperor of Rome] sought to minimize tension by merging religious celebrations, and traditions into a compromise acceptable to most. Because the Church in Rome had already reached the point of apostasy from their FIRST CENTURY beliefs and practices, it was no difficult task to accomplish the transition. It is in the nature of man to call that which is good, "evil" and likewise to call that which is evil, "good". And so, the transition from orthodoxy into Catholicized Christianity began. The exchange of Passover for Easter, the exchange of Tabernacles for Christmas, The exchange of immersion for sprinkling, the exchange of leavened bread [the Lord's Table] for the [unleavened] disc of the Sun-God and on and on. Let's take a look at Christ Mass----

Christmas

Christmas [Christ Mass] is a tradition assimilated into Christendom early in Church history. It was originally called by its pagan name, "the Venerable DAY of the SUN", and was celebrated on December 25th. In pagan culture, it was believed that the Sun God [called Rah or Mithra] became ill as the winter season grew on. The days grew shorter and shorter as the winter solstice approached which was symptomatic of the distress of Rah/Mithra. The Solstice signaled a time when the Sun God would begin his yearly recovery as the days grew longer, and there was great celebration. In the passing of time, many traditions evolved such as----

Gift giving

Singing [caroling]

❖ Evergreen trees in the home----and decorated [Jer.10;3-4]

❖ Evergreen boughs----representing the coming of spring

❖ Mistletoe----to ward off evil spirits

❖ Yule logs----to burn away evil spirits from the past

❖ Christmas bells-----heralding the death of Satan at Christ's birth [middle ages]

Santa Claus----

An ancient Norse legend, gives gifts to NICE people, rides through the air in a sleigh pulled by flying reindeer, climbs down chimneys to give presents on Christmas eve----[never gets dirty], lives in the far north---- [never gets cold], dresses funny, lives with elves who make toys, has a jolly wife who loves to bake cookies, appears in shopping malls all over America [is budgeted into mall expenses every year]. He seems to be everywhere at the same time [omnipresent?], delivers presents to billions of children all over the world [somewhere between midnight and 4 A.M. on December 25th]. Parents teach their children to believe all of this-----of course the children are disappointed when they learn they have been deceived.

So what is the purpose of Christmas? The Bible clearly tells us that every LIE is from HELL, and that Satan is the AUTHOR of LIES. Is Christmas a lie? The purpose of Christmas is akin to the many other traditions and celebrations in the Church whose eternal PURPOSE is to DILUTE the precious words of truth found in the Bible. The author of Christmas KNOWS WHAT HE IS DOING! He knows that "time" is on his side. He knows that with the passing of "time" and in repetition, anything can be accepted as truth, or at least "an acceptable practice". We are much like the children who believe in Santa, except that we do not have the honesty of

a child, and take notice of the fact that we have been deceived---
--and STOP BELIEVING IN A LIE. Christmas is a LIE!

Eph.4:25

"Wherefore putting away lying, speak every man truth with his neighbor; for we are members one of another."

Colossians 3:9-10.

"Lie not one to another, seeing that ye have put off the old man with his deeds; And have put on the new man, which is renewed in knowledge after the image of him that created him:"

Tabernacles---The Birth of Jesus

To begin with; I would like to say that Christians should NOT celebrate "Hebrew Feasts". Those celebrations were given SPECIFICALLY to the children of Jacob. Some [as in Passover] were types and foreshadows of things to come. Each year there is a gathering of the IGNORANT [Christians] in Jerusalem, to celebrate the FEAST OF TABENACLES. This is a "foolish congregation of THE FOOLISH". They violate the New Testament by attempting to integrate Old Testament Festival Laws into "Christianity". The writer of Hebrews clearly speaks to this flagrant affront to our Testament in BLOOD. The ONLY authorized sacraments of the Church are BAPTISM IN WATER, and THE LORDS TABLE! Traditionalizing into the Christian culture; a GRAB-BAG of the TRADITIONS OF MEN i.e.-----Easter----Christmas-----Ash Wednesday-----Saints' Days---
--Monthly Communions------ add to this, the American traditions of the "Church", Veterans' Day-------July 4-------Mothers' Day-
-----Fathers' Day------and most recently---9/11, has caused the Church to become an unrecognizable entity in light of the New Testament. Let me say once again-----There are only TWO authorized sacraments of the Church. They are BAPTISM shortly after conversion--------and the LORDS' TABLE at Passover. That's the way the New Testament Church celebrated their Lord for over TWO HUNDRED YEARS.

Now to the message of "TABERNACLES"; What is the significance of this day to the Church? It is the evening that Christ was born. I no longer engage in debate on this subject. The author of the third Gospel of the New Testament devotes TWO FULL CHAPTERS to the clarity of this fact. He reiterates in Chapter 3 of the book of LUKE, as he declares of Messiah at his baptism----- "and he began to be about THIRTY YEARS OF AGE"! A grade school child can count backwards "three and one half years" [the length of Christ's ministry], from that Passover that Christ was sacrificed, and land SMACK DAB-----at TABERNACLES "and Jesus began to be about thirty years old". He began to be THIRTY YEARS OLD at his baptism----AT TABERNACLES! Adding this to the splendid account of Luke chapters ONE and TWO, and the precise point in time of Messiah's birth becomes undeniable. It all hinges on one little verse in Luke chapter one---"and he [Zechariah] was of the ORDER OF ABIJAH"! The "ORDER OF ABIJAH" serves in the Temple in the SEVENTH WEEK following Passover. It was "IN THOSE DAYS" [that Zachariah finished his priestly duty], that Elizabeth [John's mother] conceived. Nine months later----John was born at Passover. Ask any Jew in the world----"when must Elijah come?", --and the answer will be the same------------"AT PASSOVER"! John [Elijah] was born at Passover! Those who wish to debate this scriptural FACT are simply REBELLIOUS-----and REJECT that information that the Lord has so abundantly provided!

In the SIXTH MONTH of Elizabeth's pregnancy; a young virgin of the tribe of Judah conceived. Counting nine months forward from the SIXTH MONTH of Elizabeth's pregnancy, brings us exactly to TABERNACLES! An easier way to account is simply to note that Miriam's baby would be born SIX MONTHS after John's birth AT PASSOVER---------which brings us exactly to TABERNACLES!

In our family, and in our fellowship, we recognize the truth about the birth of Jesus. We set aside ONE EVENING PER YEAR, to reflect on that blessed event. The moon is always full on that evening, and gives a luminous testimony of what God has done for mankind, when the "WORD BECAME FLESH AND TABERNACLED AMONG US [John 1]".

NO GAUDY TREE------NO CHEAP GIFTS---------NO CROWDED SHOPPING MALLS--------NO DEPRESSION AND SUICIDE-------- NO SANTA-----NO DRUNKENESS--------and no one to spread Satan's message to the children. Just a full moon, blessed peace, and the confident assurance that God is magnificent.

THIS MATTER WILL NOT BE SKIRTED IN THE MILLINIAL REIGN of Christ

Zech 14:15-17

15 And so shall be the plague of the horse, of the mule, of the camel, and of the ass, and of all the beasts that shall be in these tents, as this plague.

*16 And it shall come to pass, that every one that is left of all the nations which came against Jerusalem shall even go up from year to **year to worship the King, the LORD of hosts, and to keep the feast of tabernacles.***

17 And it shall be, that whoso will not come up of all the families of the earth unto Jerusalem to worship the King, the LORD of hosts, even upon them shall be no rain. KJV

THE BIRTH OF JESUS---LUKE 1-3

Windows Live™: Keep your life in sync. See how it works.

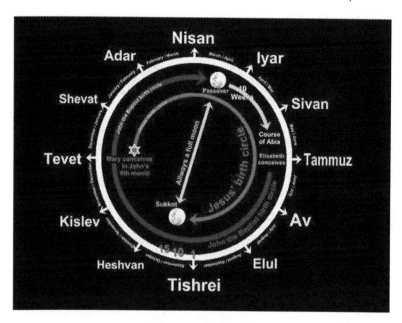

Lame EXCUSES about Christmas

I've heard it a hundred times, those lame excuses about why it is important to celebrate this lie, why it's ok to perpetuate this ancient hoax. Everybody knows it's a fake, but few are willing to confront the problem. Excuses abound. The most common excuses are perpetuated by preachers and Church leaders. It goes like this----"there are many lost souls who would never attend Church except on Christmas or Easter Sunday. It's important to reach these poor lost souls with the message of the Gospel and Christmas is a very good time to accomplish this. We use Christmas as an evangelistic tool". To this folly I would reply--------

Eph 1:3-6

3 Blessed be the God and Father of our Lord Jesus Christ, who hath blessed us with all spiritual blessings in heavenly places in Christ:

*4 **According as he hath chosen us in him before the foundation of the world**, that we should be holy and without blame before him in love:*

*5 **Having predestinated us** unto the adoption of children by Jesus Christ to himself, according to the good pleasure of his will,*

6 To the praise of the glory of his grace, wherein he hath made us accepted in the beloved.KJV

One's eternal destiny does not depend on whether or not you happen to attend a Christmas or Easter celebration. We are predestined in Christ before the foundation of the world. What need of a lie to be born again?

<u>*Eph 4:23-25*</u>

23 And be renewed in the spirit of your mind;

24 And that ye put on the new man, which after God is created in righteousness and true holiness.

*25 **Wherefore putting away lying, speak every man truth** with his neighbor: for we are members one of another. KJV*

Is Christmas the truth? If not, according to this scriptural admonition, you must "put it off" and tell the truth.

That other famous lie goes like this-------"Since the Bible does not actually TELL US when Christ was born, don't you think it important for us to have a special day to celebrate the Lord's birth?" To this I reply-----"the Bible is very clear regarding the birth of Jesus. Luke has devoted three chapters of the New Testament to the truth about the savior's birth, as I have already shown. This, just one more excuse, to perpetuate the traditions of men and to hold those traditions in higher esteem than the Word of God. It is the TRUTH that sets us free".

WHAT ABOUT EASTER?

Most Christians either DO NOT KNOW--------or DO NOT CARE, about the history of EASTER and the meanings of its varied celebrations world-wide. The history of Easter is decoded in it's very NAME. This yearly celebration is named for the ancient Babylonian goddess "ISHTAR" of the very same pronunciation [eester]. This celebration, like most ancient holy days, begins in Babylonian religious myth. In the days of ancient Babylonia, there was a renowned King by the name of Nimrod. You may remember Nimrod from the Old Testament. Nimrod was married to Ishtar. After Nimrod's death; in order to consolidate power, and to keep control in the hands of Ishtar and her son, Ishtar married her own son whose name was Tammuz. One day as Tammuz was hunting for wild boar [for he was a great hunter as was his father Nimrod], he [Tammuz] was gored by a wild pig. He became very ill from this injury and later died of his wounds. In torment, and grief, Ishtar prayed to the gods of the underworld to release her son from the bondage therein. In the mythology; the god's of the underworld agreed to release Tammuz from his captivity for one day per year. That DAY came to be known as ISHTAR , and the day of the week was that ancient weekly pagan holy day of SUN-DAY. Each year at the SUNRISE of ISHTAR SUN-DAY------all of the empire was compelled to celebrate the yearly freedom of Tammuz------but NOT WITHOUT PRECEDING TRAVAIL AND WEEPING. It was required that the WOMEN of the empire should WEEP IN TRAVAIL for FOURTY DAYS prior to Ishtar Sun-day morning. With grief satisfactory to the Lord's of the Underworld,----Tammuz was released. This became known as the "WEEPING FOR TAMMUZ". It was later Christianized into the "season of Lent". It is recorded in Ezekiel:

Ezek 8:14-18

*14 Then he brought me to the entrance to the north gate of the house of the LORD, **and I saw women sitting there, mourning for Tammuz.** 15 He said to me, "Do you see this, son of man? You will see things that are even more detestable than this."*

*16 He then brought me into the inner court of the house of the LORD, **and there at the entrance to the temple, between the portico and the altar, were about twenty-five men. With their backs toward the temple of the LORD and their faces toward the east, they were bowing down to the sun in the east.***

Danny McDowell

*17 He said to me, "Have you seen this, son of man? **Is it a trivial matter for the house of Judah to do the detestable things they are doing here?** Must they also fill the land with violence and continually provoke me to anger? Look at them putting the branch to their nose!*

18 Therefore I will deal with them in anger; I will not look on them with pity or spare them. Although they shout in my ears, I will not listen to them." NIV

In this same vein----it was a practice of the ELDERS of apostate Israel to stand with their BACKS TO THE TEMPLE and to worship the RISING OF THE SUN [Tammuz]. This abominable practice not only made its way into apostate Israel, but into the entirety of the Mediterranean world under varied local names for the goddess called ISHTAR [pronounced EESTER].

Later in time, as the Bishops of Rome [popes] contrived to unify Roman religions, and give unchallenged POWER to the Pontiff; many pagan practices were introduced to the NOW APOSTATE church. EASTER was one of MANY to find its way into Christendom. In order to "Christianize" these clearly PAGAN traditions, the church of Rome was compelled to create acceptable religious fable in order to placate the contemporary believer. Hence, we have the "LENTEN SEASON [forty days of weeping for Tammuz], and EASTER SUNDAY [the resurrection of Tammuz]. This practice is now universally celebrated in the yearly "Sunrise Service" on Easter Sun-day morning. It has nothing to do with the resurrection of Jesus. The New Testament clearly tells us that there was no such "sunrise" resurrection.

John 20:1-2

*20:1 Early on the first day of the week, **while it was still dark**, Mary Magdalene went to the tomb and saw that the stone had been removed from the entrance. 2 So she came running to Simon Peter and the other disciple, the one Jesus loved, and said, "**They have taken the Lord out of the tomb**, and we don't know where they have put him!" NIV*

128

Time has been the enemy of orthodoxy in many things. Given enough TIME and ANYTHING can be sold to an already Apostate Church.

<u>1 Timothy 4:1-2</u>

4:1 The Spirit clearly says that in later times **some will abandon the faith and follow deceiving spirits and things taught by demons.**

2 Such teachings come through hypocritical liars, whose consciences have been seared as with a hot iron.

So now we have, NOT ONLY THE HOAX-------but the hoax has become an ENTRENCHED TRADITION to the very sad realization that the entire PASSION STORY, as abundantly presented in the New Testament, has been displaced with tradition and fable. There is no need for fable. Truth will suffice.

<u>*1 Cor 5:7-8*</u>

*7 Purge out therefore the old leaven, that ye may be a new lump, as ye are unleavened. For **even Christ our passover is sacrificed for us***

8 Therefore let us keep the feast, not with old leaven, neither with the leaven of malice and wickedness; but with the unleavened bread of sincerity and truth. KJV

The New Testament is so CLEAR about this matter, that the DENIAL of these Biblical witnesses borders on that very proclamation of the Apostle Paul:

<u>*2 Thessalonians 2:9-12*</u>

10 and in every sort of evil that deceives those who are perishing. ***They perish because they refused to love the truth and so be saved.***

11 For this reason God sends them a powerful delusion so that they will believe the lie

12 and so that all will be condemned who have not believed the truth but have delighted in wickedness. NIV

Christ is our ETERNAL PASSOVER! There is NO EXCUSE for this abominable exchange that has been celebrated in the church for CENTURIES-----NONE!!

In the fourteenth day of AVIV----in the year THIRTY AD------a man hung on a STAUROS, and in the NINTH HOUR of the day he cried out ----"IT IS FINISHED". That man was the Messiah of Israel, the SAVIOR OF THE WORLD-----THE VERY SON OF GOD---------CHRIST-----------OUR PASSOVER!! He gave up the Ghost at the VERY MOMENT that the Temple HIGH PRIEST killed the yearly Passover Lamb. It was at that critical point in time that the GATES OF HELL TREMBLED. It was at that very moment that MY SINS were open to VAST ATONEMENT! It was at that very moment that the LAW became ENMITY to GRACE! It was at that moment that EVERY NAME WRITTEN IN THE BOOK OF LIFE BECAME SEALED!

What shame-------shame-- shame-- shame, that we should sacrifice the TRUTH for such a lame fable as EASTER. EASTER IS NOT PASSOVER-------and PASSOVER IS NOT EASTER. Passover falls on the FULL MOON nearest the SPRING EQUINOX [March/April]. It shall NEVER CHANGE.

For two hundred years the church followed the tradition of the Apostles and celebrated the ONLY AUTHORIZED CELEBRATION of the DEATH----BURIAL----AND RESURRECTION of the Savior. Jesus said "do this in remembrance of me". They celebrated this event ONCE PER YEAR------AT PASSOVER. It was THE LORD'S TABLE!--------THEN CAME THE BISHOPS OF ROME!

1 Cor 11:24-30

24 And when he had given thanks, he brake it, and said, Take, eat: this is my body, which is broken for you: this do in remembrance of me.

25 After the same manner also he took the cup, when he had supped, saying, This cup is the new testament in my blood: this do ye, as oft as ye drink it, in remembrance of me.

26 For as often as ye eat this bread, and drink this cup, ye do shew the Lord's death till he come.

27 Wherefore whosoever shall eat this bread, and drink this cup of the Lord, unworthily, shall be guilty of the body and blood of the Lord.

28 But let a man examine himself, and so let him eat of that bread, and drink of that cup.

29 For he that eateth and drinketh unworthily, eateth and drinketh damnation to himself, not discerning the Lord's body.

30 For this cause many are weak and sickly among you, and many sleep. KJV

Let's get straight to the point-----we were never authorized to celebrate the sacrifice of God's Son in any way other than the Lord's Table! We are commanded to celebrate the Savior's DEATH------TILL HE COMES. We celebrate Christ's death in the Lord's table. This sacrament has been lost to the paganization of our faith. It's not too late. We can fix it. All we have to do is return to the New Testament.

Just look at I Cor.11:27-----it says "whoever celebrates this sacrament unworthily is guilty of Christ's blood". That's how important this matter is. Let's try to give honor to the Sacraments by dismissing the traditions of men, and returning to the orthodoxy of the early Church.

Each year at Passover we celebrate the Lord's Table under a predictable full moon in the evening of 14 AVIV [March/April full moon]. Why not do the same? It's wonderful to know that you are following a great crowd of New Testament Saints as we celebrate "CHRIST----OUR PASSOVER".

Danny McDowell

LOOK AT THE WORDS OF HYSLOP

"The festival, of which we read in Church history, under the name of Easter, in the third or fourth centuries, was quite a different festival from that now observed in the Romish [and Protestant] Church, and at that time was not known by any such name as Easter. It was called Pasch, or the Passover, and though not of Apostolic institution [It was instituted by God and by Jesus--Lev 23; Matt 26:17-29; Mark 14:12-25; Luke 22:7-20; I Cor 11:23-30], was very early observed by many professing Christians in commemoration of the death and resurrection of Christ [It is a memorial of His death, not His resurrection--I Cor 11:26]. That festival agreed originally with the time of the Jewish [i.e., God's] Passover, when Christ was crucified . . . That festival was not idolatrous, and it was preceded by no Lent" (Alexander Hislop, The Two Babylons, p.104)

Note in this following account of the life of Polycarp; that the celebration of the New Covenant was clearly commanded to take place at Passover. Paul is recorded as insisting that this Sacrament take place YEARLY as also suggested in the New Testament.

**A disciple of John, the Apostle
(by Pionius who knew him
& witnessed his Martyrdom in A.D. 166)**

"TRACING my steps farther back, I shall begin with the visit of the blessed Paul to Smyrna, as I found it in ancient copies. I will give the following narration in order, thereby coming down to the history of the blessed Polycarp.

2. In the days of unleavened bread, Paul, came down from Galatia, and arrived in Asia. He considered the peacefulness among the faithful in Smyrna to be a great refreshment in Christ Jesus, after his severe toil. He then intended afterwards to depart to Jerusalem.

In Smyrna he went to visit Strataeas (who had listened to him in Pamphylia) who was the son of Eunice the daughter of Lois. These are they whom he mentions when writing to Timothy, saying, "Of the unfeigned faith that is in you, which dwelt first in thy grandmother

132

Lois and in thy mother Eunice" (2 Tim. 1:5). Consequently, we find that Stratæas was Timothy's brother.

Paul then, entering his house and gathering together the faithful there, spoke to them concerning the Passover and the Pentecost. He reminded them of the New Covenant of the offering of bread and the cup. He stated how they ought, most assuredly, to celebrate it during the days of unleavened bread, holding fast to the new mystery of the Passion (literally-Christ's sufferings) and Resurrection. It is here that the Apostle plainly teaches that we ought not to keep it outside the season of unleavened bread, as the heretics do, especially the Phrygians. Also, on the other hand, not necessarily on the fourteenth day, either. Paul said nothing about the fourteenth day, but only named the days of unleavened bread, the Passover, and the Pentecost, thus confirming the Gospel.

3. After the Apostle left, Stratæas continued to spread his teaching, as well as others after him. These other's, and their names, will I mention later concerning their manner of life, in as much as it is possible to know. But for the present, let us proceed to the subject of Polycarp.

THE BREAD OF THE NEW COVENANT

NT:740---bread

artos (ar'-tos); from NT:142; bread (as raised) or a loaf:

KJV - (shew-) bread, loaf.

In every reference of the New Testament regarding the BREAD of the NEW COVENANT, the Greek word ARTOS is used exclusively. There is a very PERTINENT REASON for the use of this word "ARTOS". I will discuss this reasoning as we continue this study.

ARTOS

Matt 4:3-5

3 And when the tempter came to him, he said, If thou be the Son of God, command that these stones be made **bread [artos]**.

4 But he answered and said, It is written, Man shall not live **by bread [artos]** alone, but by every word that proceedeth out of the mouth of God. KJV

Matt 7:9-10

9 Or what man is there of you, whom if his son **ask bread [artos]**, will he give him a stone? KJV

Matt 16:7-9

7 And they reasoned among themselves, saying, It is because we have taken no **bread [artos]**.

8 Which when Jesus perceived, he said unto them, O ye of little faith, why reason ye among yourselves, because ye have brought no **bread [artos]**? KJV

Mark 6:36-38

36 Send them away, that they may go into the country round about, and into the villages, and buy themselves **bread [artos]**: for they have nothing to eat.

37 He answered and said unto them, Give ye them to eat. And they say unto him, Shall we go and buy two hundred pennyworth **of bread [artos]**, and give them to eat?

Mark 14:22-23

22 And as they did eat, **Jesus took bread [ARTOS]**, and blessed, and brake it, and gave to them, and said, Take, eat: **this is my body**.

Luke 22:19-20

*19 And he took **bread [ARTOS]**, and gave thanks, and brake it, and gave unto them, saying, This is my body which is given for you: this do in remembrance of me.*

Mark 14;22;23

*This is the **BREAD [ARTOS]** of the New Covenant. In every reference to the Lord's Table----THIS WORD "ARTOS" is used without exception. It is a loaf.*

This following use of the word "bread" is clearly a translation from the Greek word "ARTOS". This was an un-ceremonial "bread". It was leavened bread.

Luke 24:30-36

*30 And it came to pass, as he sat at meat with them, **he took bread [artos]**, and blessed it, and brake, and gave to them.*

31 And their eyes were opened, and they knew him; and he vanished out of their sight.

32 And they said one to another, Did not our heart burn within us, while he talked with us by the way, and while he opened to us the scriptures?

33 And they rose up the same hour, and returned to Jerusalem, and found the eleven gathered together, and them that were with them,

34 Saying, The Lord is risen indeed, and hath appeared to Simon.

*35 And they told what things were done in the way, and how he was known of them **in breaking of bread [artos] KJV***

Notice in the following, the vital connection between BREAD and WINE in this familiar COMMUNION PASSAGE.

Luke 22:19-21

*19 **And he took bread [artos]**, and gave thanks, and brake it, and gave unto them, saying, This is my body which is given for you: this do in remembrance of me.*

*20 Likewise also the cup after supper, saying, **This cup is the new testament in my blood, which is shed for you.** KJV*

THE BREAKING OF BREAD WITHOUT THE COMMUNION CUP IS SIMPLY A COMMUNAL MEAL AND HAS NO RELEVANCE TO THE LORD'S TABLE! The word "artos" is used in both.

Acts 20;7-11

*7 And upon the first day of the week, **when the disciples came together to break bread [artos]**, Paul preached unto them, ready to depart on the morrow; and continued his speech until midnight.*

8 And there were many lights in the upper chamber, where they were gathered together.

9 And there sat in a window a certain young man named Eutychus, being fallen into a deep sleep: and as Paul was long preaching, he sunk down with sleep, and fell down from the third loft, and was taken up dead.

10 And Paul went down, and fell on him, and embracing him said, Trouble not yourselves; for his life is in him.

*11 When he therefore was come up again, **and broken bread [artos]**, and eaten, and had talked a long while, even till break of day, so he departed **KJV***

Some insist that this "breaking of bread" was the ceremonial TABLE OF THE LORD in every instance where people came together for a meal simply because they "broke bread" together. A simple exercise in logic should dismiss such a notion.

Take a close look at this clearly defined *TABLE OF THE LORD!*

<u>Cor 10:16-18</u>

16 The cup of blessing which we bless, is it not the communion of the blood of Christ? **The bread [artos] which we break, is it not the communion of the body of Christ?**

17 For we being many are one bread, and one body: for we **are all partakers of that one bread [artos].**

The evidence is very clear. The Lord's Table was always celebrated with leavened bread [artos]. The leaven in the bread represented OUR SINS which God had laid on Christ to be remitted at the CROSS. This is the manner in which the early Church celebrated the Lord's Table until it was corrupted by the Roman WAFER----embossed with a sunburst, a tribute to the day of the Sun, i.e.----Sun worship. In every passage in the New Testament where "ceremonial bread" was used, it is translated from the Greek word AZUMOS [unleavened bread----Passover bread]. That word AZUMOS is never used in regard to the Lord's Table----NOT ONCE We have drifted so far from our beginnings.

<u>1 Cor 11:23-31</u>

23 For I have received of the Lord that which also I delivered unto you, That the Lord Jesus the same night in which he was betrayed took bread **[artos]:**

24 And when he had given thanks, he brake it, and said, Take, eat: this is my body, which is broken for you: this do in remembrance of me.

25 After the same manner also he took the cup, **when he had supped, saying, This cup is the new testament in my blood: this do ye, as oft as ye drink it, in remembrance of me.**

26 For as often as ye eat this bread **[artos],** *and drink this cup, ye do shew the Lord's death till he come.*

27 Wherefore whosoever shall eat this bread **[artos],** *and drink this cup of the Lord, unworthily, shall be guilty of the body and blood of the Lord.*

28 But let a man examine himself, and so let him eat of that bread, and drink of that cup.

29 For he that eateth and drinketh unworthily, eateth and drinketh damnation to himself, not discerning the Lord's body.

30 For this cause many are weak and sickly among you, and many sleep.

THE CREMONIAL BREAD

AZUMOS

NT:106

azumos (ad'-zoo-mos); from NT:1 (as a negative particle) and NT:2219; unleavened, i.e. (figuratively) uncorrupted; (in the neutral plural) specially (by implication) the Passover week:

KJV - unleavened (bread).

This is the "CEREMONIAL BREAD" of Passover. This is UNLEAVENED bread. Furthermore-----this UNLEAVENED BREAD is NEVER used in reference to the "BREAD" of the New Covenant------*NOT ONCE!*

Matt 26:17-22

*17 Now the first day of the feast of **unleavened bread [AZUMOS]** the disciples came to Jesus, saying unto him, Where wilt thou that we prepare for thee to eat the **Passover**?*

18 And he said, Go into the city to such a man, and say unto him, The Master saith, My time is at hand; I will keep the Passover at thy house with my disciples.

19 And the disciples did as Jesus had appointed them; and they made ready the Passover.

20 Now when the even was come, he sat down with the twelve.

21 And as they did eat, he said, Verily I say unto you, that one of you shall betray me.

We must clarify that Jesus was NOT serving the "Passover" on this evening----but rather, was beginning the PREPARATION [the Day of Preparation] for the Passover. This was the evening of 13/14 Aviv-------the day the Passover would be killed. The FOLLOWING EVENING [Nisan Aviv 14/15] would begin the Passover----the "Days of UNLEAVENED BREAD".

Nisan Aviv 13/14

<u>Matt 26:26-27</u>

*26 And as they were eating, Jesus took **bread [ARTOS]**, and blessed it, and brake it, and gave it to the disciples, and said, Take, eat; **this is my body.** KJV*

Luke 22:1-8

*22:1 Now the feast of **unleavened bread [AZUMOS]** drew nigh, which is called the Passover.*

2 And the chief priests and scribes sought how they might kill him; for they feared the people.

3 Then entered Satan into Judas surnamed Iscariot, being of the number of the twelve.

4 And he went his way, and communed with the chief priests and captains, how he might betray him unto them.

5 And they were glad, and covenanted to give him money.

6 And he promised, and sought opportunity to betray him unto them in the absence of the multitude.

*7 Then came the day of **unleavened bread [azumos], when the Passover must be killed.** KJV*

1 Cor 5:8-9

*8 Therefore **let us keep the feast**, not with old leaven, neither with the leaven of malice and wickedness; **but with the unleavened bread [azumos] of sincerity and truth.***

In Paul's plea for the "unleavened bread of sincerity" in this passage; some would attempt to utilize this phrase "unleavened bread" to justify the use of AZUMOS [unleavened bread] in celebration of the Lord's Table, however, Strong's reference 9999 clearly tells us the KJV translators added the word "BREAD" to the passage for their own understanding in the sentence, and that NO SUCH WORD [bread] EXISTS in the original language of this passage. Therefore, when Paul refers to "entering the FEAST" [the Lord's Table at Passover] he simply states-----"let us keep the feast [the Lord's Table] with the "UNLEAVEN OF SINCERITY AND TRUTH"-----and NEVER SUGGESTS that unleavened bread should be used in the Lord's table. The only use of the word "leaven" is in typology to our own sins, and is admonished to be PURGED FROM OUR CONCIENCE prior to our participation in the BODY and BLOOD of JESUS.

May we now come to the CRUX of this study. What does it matter that we celebrate the Lord's Table this way or that? Would you not agree that so many of our beliefs and celebrations have been corrupted in the passage of TIME? Have we no ENEMY to steal at opportune times? Is IGNORANCE truly a virtue? Are we AGENTS OF TRADITION? What is the importance of ORTHODOXY in this matter? May I take you to Isaiah 53:

"FOR THE LORD HATH LAID UPON HIM THE INIQUITIES [leaven] OF US ALL"

This is the MATTER for us. The leaven of SIN was placed upon Christ-------OUR SIN! That's why it is important to *RESIST the TRADITIONS OF MEN, and to HOLD FAST to the teachings of the New Testament. We celebrate the Lord's table yearly at Passover-------as did the New Testament Church for nearly TWO*

HUNDRED YEARS following that initial Table set by our Master. It's important-----It really is! It's important to recognize that -------OUR SIN [leaven]--------was laid upon him! Look what we have lost with the passing of time. Look at how time and TRADITION have buried the truth.

In the 17th century the Catholic Church held the Council of Trent to rebut and address criticisms of the Reformation Movement. In the fourth session, the council determined that "Church Tradition" held equal authority to Scripture, whereas the Reformers concluded that Scripture Alone [Sola Scriptura] held authority in all things concerning the Church. Unfortunately, the banner of Sola Scriptura has been soiled by many unauthorized doctrines and practices within the Protestant Church. It remains so today.

CHAPTER VI

WHO ARE YOU?

There has rarely been an occasion when I have NOT heard this awful Sunday morning greeting at "Church". "Good morning every one. Are you glad to be in God's House today? Wouldn't you rather be in God's House than the best Hospital or Jail in town? Isn't it wonderful that we can meet at God's House and expect wonderful things from the Lord, yada yada yada". Sarcastically, I'm saying to myself---"I'm sure glad the Lord has such a nice place to stay". Innocent though this greeting may seem, in actuality, it is deeply heretical and in no way reflects the image of "God's House" portrayed in the New Testament. I have heard the song, "we are standing on Holy Ground", and in my mind I am thinking "this Holy Ground could use a good carpet cleaner". It's all very moving , but is it Biblical? Let's see what the New Testament has to say about God's House.

THE HOUSE OF GOD

THE TEMPLE OF GOD

<u>1 Cor 3:9-18</u>

9 For we are labourers together with God: ye are God's husbandry, ye are God's building.

10 According to the grace of God which is given unto me, as a wise masterbuilder, I have laid the foundation, and another buildeth thereon. **But let every man take heed how he buildeth thereupon.**

11 For other foundation can no man lay than that is laid, which is Jesus Christ.

12 **Now if any man build upon this foundation** gold, silver, precious stones, wood, hay, stubble;

13 Every man's work shall be made manifest: for the day shall declare it, because it shall be revealed by fire; and the fire shall try every man's work of what sort it is.

14 If any man's work abide **which he hath built thereupon**, he shall receive a reward.

15 If any man's work shall be burned, he shall suffer loss: but he himself shall be saved; yet so as by fire.

16 **Know ye not that ye are the temple of God, and that the Spirit of God dwelleth in you?**

17 If any man defile the temple of God, him shall God destroy; for the temple of God is holy, **which temple ye are.**

1 Cor 6:19-7:1

19 What? know ye not that **your body is the temple of the Holy Ghost** which is in you, which ye have of God, and ye are not your own?

20 For ye are bought with a price: therefore glorify God in your body, and in your spirit, which are God's.

Eph 2:19-22

19 Now therefore ye are no more strangers and foreigners, but fellow citizens with the saints, **and of the household of God;**

20 And are built upon the foundation of the apostles and prophets, **Jesus Christ himself being the chief corner stone;**

21 In whom all the building fitly framed together groweth unto **an holy temple in the Lord**:

22 In whom ye also are builded together **for an habitation of God through the Spirit.**

The House of God

1 Tim 3:14-16

14 These things write I unto thee, hoping to come unto thee shortly:

15 But if I tarry long, that thou mayest know how thou oughtest to behave thyself **in the house of God, which is the church of the living God**, the pillar and ground of the truth.

Heb 10:20-24

20 By a new and living way, which he hath consecrated for us, through the veil, that is to say, his flesh;

21 And having an high priest over **the house of God;**

22 Let us draw near with a true heart in full assurance of faith, having our hearts sprinkled from an evil conscience, and our bodies washed with pure water.

23 Let us hold fast the profession of our faith without wavering; (for he is faithful that promised;)

1 Peter 4:17-18

17 For the time is come that judgment must begin **at the house of God: and if it first begin at us,** what shall the end be of them that obey not the gospel of God?

THE CHURCH

Romans 15;5

5 Likewise, **greet the church that is in their house.** Salute my wellbeloved Epaenetus, who is the firstfruits of Achaia unto Christ.

6 Greet Mary, who bestowed much labour on us.

7 Salute Andronicus and Junia, my kinsmen, and my fellow prisoners, who are of note among the apostles, who also were in Christ before me.

8 Greet Amplias my beloved in the Lord.

9 Salute Urbane, our helper in Christ, and Stachys my beloved.

10 Salute Apelles approved in Christ. Salute them which are of Aristobulus' household.

11 Salute Herodion my kinsman. Greet them that be of the household of Narcissus, which are in the Lord.

12 Salute Tryphena and Tryphosa, who labour in the Lord. Salute the beloved Persis, which laboured much in the Lord.

13 Salute Rufus chosen in the Lord, and his mother and mine.

14 Salute Asyncritus, Phlegon, Hermas, Patrobas, Hermes, and the brethren which are with them.

15 Salute Philologus, and Julia, Nereus, and his sister, and Olympas, and all the saints which are with them.

16 Salute one another with an holy kiss. **The churches of Christ salute you.**

1 Cor 16:15-20

15 I beseech you, brethren, (ye know the house of Stephanas, that it is the firstfruits of Achaia, and that they have addicted themselves to the ministry of the saints,)

16 That ye submit yourselves unto such, and to everyone that helpeth with us, and laboureth.

17 I am glad of the coming of Stephanas and Fortunatus and Achaicus: for that which was lacking on your part they have supplied.

18 For they have refreshed my spirit and yours: therefore acknowledge ye them that are such.

*19 **The churches of Asia salute you**. Aquila and Priscilla salute you much in the Lord, with the church that is in their house.*

Col 4:15 - 1 Thess 1:1

*15 Salute the brethren which are in Laodicea, and Nymphas, **and the church which is in his house.***

*16 And when this epistle is read among you, cause that it **be read also in the church of the Laodiceans**; and that ye likewise read the epistle from Laodicea.*

17 And say to Archippus, Take heed to the ministry which thou hast received in the Lord, that thou fulfil it.

18 The salutation by the hand of me Paul. Remember my bonds. Grace be with you. Amen.

Philem 2-4

*2 And to our beloved Apphia, and Archippus our fellow soldier, **and to the church in thy house:***

3 Grace to you, and peace, from God our Father and the Lord Jesus Christ.

Heb 3:4-7

4 For every house is builded by some man; but he that built all things is God.

5 And Moses verily was faithful in all his house, as a servant, for a testimony of those things which were to be spoken after;

6 But Christ as a son over his own house; **whose house are we**, if we hold fast the confidence and the rejoicing of the hope firm unto the end.

CONTEMPT FOR GOD'S HOUSE

Heb 6:4-6

4 For it is impossible for those who were once enlightened, and have tasted of the heavenly gift, and were made partakers of the Holy Ghost,

5 And have tasted the good word of God, and the powers of the world to come,

6 If they shall fall away, to renew them again unto repentance; seeing they crucify to themselves the Son of God afresh, and put him to an open shame.

Heb 10:29-30

29 Of how much sorer punishment, suppose ye, shall he be thought worthy, who hath trodden underfoot the Son of God, and hath counted the blood of the covenant, wherewith he was sanctified, an unholy thing, and hath done despite unto the Spirit of grace?

Matt 24:2

2 And Jesus said unto them, See ye not all these things? verily I say unto you, There shall not be left here one stone upon another, that shall not be thrown down.

2 Cor 6:16

16 And what agreement **hath the temple of God** with idols? **for ye are the temple of the living God**; as God hath said, **I will dwell in them, and walk in them; and I will be their God, and they shall be my people.**

Some will ask, "what difference does it make? How important is it really? Aren't you just splitting hairs? We all know what the New Testament says about the Temple of God, and the House of God----we know that. I just don't see that it is that important, after all---didn't' God give us this wonderful building that we worship in? Isn't it OK to refer to this place as HOLY GROUND? After all---this building is dedicated to God". To those who feel this way I would just say---A great price was paid for the honor of being able to say "I am the Temple of the Holy Ghost". I am infinitely more important than the most beautiful house of worship in the world. That BUILDING can claim no relationship with my Savior. It has no soul. It has no breath. No one gave his life for it. It is not chosen in him before the foundation of the earth. It is not now, nor ever will be--- eternal. It still needs a MAN within it to spread the Gospel. When the trumpet sounds, it will burn. It does not walk nor talk. The Spirit of God does not live there. When I walk into the building---the TEMPLE OF GOD HAS ARRIVED, and when I leave----THE TEMPLE OF GOD HAS DEPARTED. There is no other TEMPLE OF GOD! It does not exist!"

BUILDING PROJECTS

The absolute OBSESSION with BUILDING PROJECTS has left the Body of Christ impoverished and enslaved to the dreams of men seeking their own VISION. Pastors, and Church leaders pitch a sell within God's House to extract the funds needed to construct their own empires. Little concern is paid to the consequences of BEATING GOD'S SHEEP! These men, seeking REPUTATION and personal FINANCIAL GAIN, are using "the redeemed of the Lord" as PACK MULES and ASSES to carry the load for their own exaltation. They are leading the people of God into the bondage of modern day Pharaoh's. Can you imagine? A great PRICE was paid in RIGHTEOUS BLOOD for the redemption of God's Elect, only to be led back to Egypt to labor in the construction of modern day PYRAMIDS---Sepulchers filled with the bones of the APOSTATE.

A cleansing is taking place in America. Huge and expensive "BUILDING PROJECTS" have been STOPPED IN THEIR TRACKS because of the economic fiascos of the RICH. When you DANCE WITH THE DEVIL, HE WILL STEP ON YOUR FEET! That is what is happening in the world of Mega Churches here in America. Bankruptcies abound, and "WORD OF FAITH" late comers are falling like dominoes. Multi-million dollar building complexes are standing empty in the wind and rain giving credence to that declaration "the foolish man built his house upon SAND". God is laughing at them. They beg for His attention, but Heaven is a BRASS WALL against them. God's people are weeping for Egypt and cannot understand why their mourning falls on deaf ears.

If you are frustrated, if no matter how much you pray and fast, weep and wail, agonize and question the Almighty because he REFUSES to allow your plans to come to fruition----it's time for you to fall to prostration and GIVE THANKS for God's grace. It's time to come to your senses and realize that God is STEARING YOU AWAY from Egypt just because he is MERCIFUL. Why, as Paul, are you KICKING AGAINST THE THORNS? Don't you see what is happening? Don't you see that you have been beguiled? Don't you understand that "building another MEGA CHURCH" is not God's priority for his people?

I say with all the truth and sincerity that is within me---- ENCUMBERING GOD'S PEOPLE WITH DEBT IS NOT FROM GOD! STOP WHAT YOU ARE TRYING TO DO-----STOP IT NOW before it's too late. The LENDER will not understand when you tell him that you cannot meet the next MORTGAGE PAYMENT on that TEMPLE OF GREED! He will repossess the land and you will be in worst financial condition than at the first and the sheep will be scattered. Be satisfied with what God has given you.

Most will ignore this plea because they just cannot turn from their "dream, their vision", but this is not God's vision for his people. God's vision for his people is for them to flourish----free from encumbrance to a building.

CHAPTER VII

THE SUPERIORITY OF GRACE

Please read this last book of the Old Testament with absolute honesty. I have highlighted the pertinent words and phrases to make this a quick and easy reading. It will only take you a few minutes,

It is the unscrupulous habit and rank dishonesty of Church leaders to present these four chapters of the Old Testament as God's will for the CHURCH. Note that throughout these four chapters of Malachi, it is clear that the Lord is speaking to the Priests and Levites of Israel. Any other representation is simply dishonest, but no problem to the Church leaders of today. They have sown in corruption and they will one day reap their harvest.

Malachi 1

*1:1 The burden of the word of the LORD to **Israel** by Malachi.*

*2 I have loved you, saith the LORD. Yet ye say, Wherein hast thou loved us? Was not Esau Jacob's brother? saith the LORD: **yet I loved Jacob,***

3 And I hated Esau, and laid his mountains and his heritage waste for the dragons of the wilderness.

4 Whereas Edom saith, We are impoverished, but we will return and build the desolate places; thus saith the LORD of hosts, They

shall build, but I will throw down; and they shall call them, The border of wickedness, and, The people against whom the LORD hath indignation forever.

5 And your eyes shall see, and ye shall say, The LORD will be magnified **from the border of Israel.**

6 A son honoureth his father, and a servant his master: if then I be a father, where is mine honour? and if I be a master, where is my fear? saith the LORD of hosts unto you, **O priests, that despise my name. And ye say, Wherein have we despised thy name?**

7 Ye offer polluted bread upon mine altar; and ye say, Wherein have we polluted thee? In that ye say, The table of the LORD is contemptible.

8 And if ye offer **the blind for sacrifice**, is it not evil? and if ye offer **the lame and sick, is it not evil**? offer it now unto thy governor; will he be pleased with thee, or accept thy person? saith the LORD of hosts.

9 And now, I pray you, beseech God that he will be gracious unto us: this hath been by your means: will he regard your persons? saith the LORD of hosts.

10 Who is there even among you that would shut the doors for nought? **neither do ye kindle fire on mine altar for nought**. I have no pleasure in you, saith the LORD of hosts, neither will I accept an offering at your hand.

11 For from the rising of the sun even unto the going down of the same **my name shall be great among the Gentiles**; and in every place incense shall be offered unto my name, and a pure offering: for my name shall be great among the heathen, saith the LORD of hosts.

12 But ye have profaned it, in that ye say, The table of the LORD is polluted; and the fruit thereof, even his meat, is contemptible.

13 Ye said also, Behold, what a weariness is it! and ye have snuffed at it, saith the LORD of hosts; **at which was torn, and the lame, and**

the sick; *thus ye brought an offering: should I accept this of your hand? saith the LORD.*

14 *But cursed be the deceiver,* **which hath in his flock a male, and voweth, and sacrificeth unto the LORD a corrupt thing**: *for I am a great King, saith the LORD of hosts, and my name is dreadful among the heathen.*

<u>Malachi 2</u>

2:1 **And now, O ye priests, this commandment is for you.**

2 *If ye will not hear, and if ye will not lay it to heart, to give glory unto my name, saith the LORD of hosts, I will even send a curse upon you, and I will curse your blessings: yea, I have cursed them already, because ye do not lay it to heart.*

3 *Behold, I will corrupt your seed, and spread dung upon your faces,* **even the dung of your solemn feasts**; *and one shall take you away with it.*

4 *And ye shall know that I have sent this commandment unto you,* **that my covenant might be with Levi, saith the LORD of hosts.**

5 *My covenant was with him of life and peace; and I gave them to him for the fear wherewith he feared me, and was afraid before my name.*

6 *The law of truth was in his mouth, and iniquity was not found in his lips: he walked with me in peace and equity, and did turn many away from iniquity.*

7 **For the priest's lips should keep knowledge, and they should seek the law at his mouth: for he is the messenger of the LORD of hosts.**

8 *But ye are departed out of the way; ye have caused many to stumble at the law;* **ye have corrupted the covenant of Levi**, *saith the LORD of hosts.*

*9 Therefore have I also made you contemptible and base before all the people, according as ye have not kept my ways, **but have been partial in the law.***

*10 Have we not all one father? hath not one God created us? why do we deal treacherously every man against his brother, **by profaning the covenant of our fathers?***

11 Judah hath dealt treacherously, and an abomination is committed in Israel and in Jerusalem; for Judah hath profaned the holiness of the LORD which he loved, and hath married the daughter of a strange god.

*12 The LORD will cut off the man that doeth this, the master and the scholar, out **of the tabernacles of Jacob**, and him that offereth an offering unto the LORD of hosts.*

13 And this have ye done again, covering the altar of the LORD with tears, with weeping, and with crying out, insomuch that he regardeth not the offering any more, or receiveth it with good will at your hand.

14 Yet ye say, Wherefore? Because the LORD hath been witness between thee and the wife of thy youth, against whom thou hast dealt treacherously: yet is she thy companion, and the wife of thy covenant.

15 And did not he make one? Yet had he the residue of the spirit. And wherefore one? That he might seek a godly seed. Therefore take heed to your spirit, and let none deal treacherously against the wife of his youth.

16 For the LORD, the God of Israel, saith that he hateth putting away: for one covereth violence with his garment, saith the LORD of hosts: therefore take heed to your spirit, that ye deal not treacherously.

17 Ye have wearied the LORD with your words. Yet ye say, Wherein have we wearied him? When ye say, Every one that doeth evil is good in the sight of the LORD, and he delighteth in them; or, Where is the God of judgment?

Malachi 3

3:1 Behold, I will send my messenger, and he shall prepare the way before me: and the Lord, whom ye seek, shall suddenly come to this temple, even the messenger of the covenant, whom ye delight in: behold, he shall come, saith the LORD of hosts.

2 But who may abide the day of his coming? and who shall stand when he appeareth? for he is like a refiner's fire, and like fullers' soap:

*3 And he shall sit as a refiner and purifier of silver: and he shall **purify the sons of Levi,** and purge them as gold and silver, that they may offer unto the LORD an offering in righteousness.*

*4 **Then shall the offering of Judah and Jerusalem be pleasant unto the LORD, as in the days of old, and as in former years.***

5 And I will come near to you to judgment; and I will be a swift witness against the sorcerers, and against the adulterers, and against false swearers, and against those that oppress the hireling in his wages, the widow, and the fatherless, and that turn aside the stranger from his right, and fear not me, saith the LORD of hosts.

*6 For I am the LORD, I change not; **therefore ye sons of Jacob** are not consumed.*

*7 Even from the days of your fathers **ye are gone away from mine ordinances,** and have not kept them. Return unto me, and I will return unto you, saith the LORD of hosts. But ye said, Wherein shall we return?*

*8 **Will a man rob God? Yet ye have robbed me. But ye say, Wherein have we robbed thee? In tithes and offerings.***

*9 Ye are cursed with a curse: for ye have robbed me, **even this whole nation.***

*10 Bring ye all the tithes **into the storehouse**, that there may be meat **in mine house**, and prove me now herewith, saith the LORD of* hosts, *if I will not open you the windows of heaven, and pour you out a blessing, that there shall not be room enough to receive it.*

*11 And I will rebuke the devourer for your sakes, and **he shall not destroy the fruits of your ground; neither shall your vine cast her fruit before the time in the field,** saith the LORD of hosts.*

12 And all nations shall call you blessed: for ye shall be a delightsome land, saith the LORD of hosts.

13 Your words have been stout against me, saith the LORD. Yet ye say, What have we spoken so much against thee?

14 Ye have said, It is vain to serve God: and what profit is it that we have kept his ordinance, and that we have walked mournfully before the LORD of hosts?

15 And now we call the proud happy; yea, they that work wickedness are set up; yea, they that tempt God are even delivered.

16 Then they that feared the LORD spake often one to another: and the LORD hearkened, and heard it, and a book of remembrance was written before him for them that feared the LORD, and that thought upon his name.

17 And they shall be mine, saith the LORD of hosts, in that day when I make up my jewels; and I will spare them, as a man spareth his own son that serveth him.

18 Then shall ye return, and discern between the righteous and the wicked, between him that serveth God and him that serveth him not.

<u>Malachi 4</u>

4:1 For, behold, the day cometh, that shall burn as an oven; and all the proud, yea, and all that do wickedly, shall be stubble: and the day that cometh shall burn them up, saith the LORD of hosts, that it shall leave them neither root nor branch.

Danny McDowell

2 But unto you that fear my name shall the Sun of righteousness arise with healing in his wings; and ye shall go forth, and grow up as calves of the stall.

3 And ye shall tread down the wicked; for they shall be ashes under the soles of your feet in the day that I shall do this, saith the LORD of hosts.

*4 **Remember ye the law of Moses my servant,** which I commanded unto him in Horeb for all Israel, with the statutes and judgments.*

5 Behold, I will send you Elijah the prophet before the coming of the great and dreadful day of the LORD:

6 And he shall turn the heart of the fathers to the children, and the heart of the children to their fathers, lest I come and smite the earth with a curse.

First, I would like you to notice that there is not ONE SINGLE mention of MONEY in the book of Malachi. As a matter of fact, there is NOWHERE in the Old Testament, a mention of "money" regarding the Tithe-----except to say, if an Israelite had too much tithe to carry to the Temple, he could SELL HIS TITHE, take the money to the place of sacrifice, PURCHASE back the same volume of food products that he had sold, and pay his tithe! The "tithe," under the law, was restricted to those who earned their living in animal husbandry or agriculture. The tithe was ALWAYS an eatable product, even to the point of tithing HERBS such as MINT and CUMMIN. The Tithe was for the provision of FOOD and DRINK for the Priesthood, and for the FEASTS of Israel. There are some, who in desperation upon learning this fact, will claim that the tribes of Israel had no "coin" [money] in those days, so the Lord required agricultural items till a monetary system should later be developed. This is pure POPPYCOCK! Coin/MONEY has been used since the times preceding Abraham. ANYTHING----- to hold on to their folly.

Tithe in itself is a display of FAITHLESSNESS. Those who coerce the Tithe simply do not have the RAW FAITH it takes to believe that God can provide WITHOUT THE TITHE. Their entire system is

156

rooted in faithlessness. It's own power lies in fear and coercion. It is akin to WITCHCRAFT. It is the same coercion that the Witch Doctors of Africa use to coerce money from the fearful. The only difference is that the Tithe is neatly wrapped in the Name of GOD. God hates it, for it diminishes the value of the CROSS! Don't you get it?----IT IS FINISHED!

Matt 23:23-24

23 Woe unto you, scribes and Pharisees, hypocrites! **for ye pay tithe of mint and anise and cummin,** *and have omitted the weightier matters of the law, judgment, mercy, and faith: these ought ye to have done, and not to leave the other undone.*

24 Ye blind guides, which strain at a gnat, and swallow a camel. KJV

Luke 11:42

42 But woe unto you, Pharisees! for ye tithe mint and rue and all manner of herbs, and pass over judgment and the love of God: these ought ye to have done, and not to leave the other undone. KJV

These words of Jesus were directed to JEWS living under the Old Covenant, for the "reconciliation for sin" had not yet come to Israel. Those who teach the TITHE as a New Testament concept may well keep company with those of whom it is said------

1 Cor 3:16-17

16 Know ye not that ye are the temple of God, and that the Spirit of God dwelleth in you?

17 If any man defile the temple of God, him shall God destroy; for the temple of God is holy, which temple ye are.

Those who teach and coerce the TITHE are defiling God's Temple. They exhume the LAW from its grave, and forcefully mingle it with Grace, resulting in a putrid religious brew condemned by the New Covenant. Those Christianized WITCH DOCTORS, called "Pastor", shove it down the throats of mindless PEW SHEEP who bleat for more-----baaaah---bah---baaaaah.

"ENMITY"-----that's what the New Testament calls it-----"ENMITY WITH GRACE".

NT:2189-----enmity

echthra (ekh'-thrah); feminine of NT:2190; hostility; by implication, a reason for opposition:

KJV - enmity, hatred.

Eph 2:15-3:1

15 *Having abolished in his flesh the enmity, even the law of commandments contained in ordinances*; *for to make in himself of twain one new man, so making peace;*

16 *And that he might reconcile both unto God in one body by the cross,* *having slain the enmity thereby:*

17 *And came and preached peace to you which were afar off, and to them that were nigh.*

18 *For through him we both have access by one Spirit unto the Father.*

19 *Now therefore ye are no more strangers and foreigners, but fellow citizens with the saints, and of the household of God;*

20 *And are built upon the foundation of the apostles and prophets, Jesus Christ himself being the chief corner stone;*

21 *In whom all the building fitly framed together groweth unto an holy temple in the Lord:*

22 In whom ye also are builded together for an habitation of God through the Spirit. KJV

<u>Heb 6:4-6</u>

*4 For it is impossible **for those who were once enlightened**, and have tasted of the heavenly gift, and were made partakers of the Holy Ghost,*

5 And have tasted the good word of God, and the powers of the world to come,

6 If they shall fall away, to renew them again unto repentance; seeing they crucify to themselves the Son of God afresh, and put him to an open shame.

<u>2 Cor 9:6-11</u>

*6 But this I say, He which soweth sparingly shall reap also sparingly; **and he which soweth bountifully shall reap also bountifully.***

*7 **Every man according as he purposeth in his heart, so let him give; not grudgingly, or of necessity: for God loveth a cheerful giver.***

- ❖ **"OR OF NECCESITY"**

*8 **And God is able to make all grace abound toward you**; that ye, always having all sufficiency in all things, may abound to every good work:*

9(As it is written, He hath dispersed abroad; he hath given to the poor: his righteousness remaineth forever.

*10 **Now he that ministereth seed to the sower both minister bread for your food, and multiply your seed sown, and increase the fruits of your righteousness;)***

11 Being enriched in everything to all bountifulness, which causeth through us thanksgiving to God.

THE INSUFFICIECY OF THE CROSS?

The New Testament is CLEAR about this matter of "giving". It is a matter of THE HEART. Paul tells us time and again, that we are to give as the Lord [through the Holy Spirit], leads us. Time and again, PASTORS smother us with promises of PROSPERITY, and more importantly------GOD'S FAVOR in the tithe. "God will FIX ANYTHING in your life, IF YOU FAITHFULLY TITHE". This is what we are told. The Body, and Blood of Jesus have become irrelevant to our privilege in the work of Christ. "There is ANOTHER path to God's favor" [they say]--------it's called THE TITHE. With it; the sacrifice of the cross becomes enhanced. Our redemption is "INCOMPLETE" without THE TITHE [they say]"! We are INDEED REDEEMED to that point where our FINANCIAL NEED comes into play--------then our Great Redeemer becomes weak, and inadequate to save" [they suggest]. "Who will save us from our financial despair?------------"THE LAW"---------THE LAW WILL SAVE US in the inadequacy of Christ's Blood" [they say]. If you will only TITHE----------then blessings are just beyond the next bend in the road. Your salvation is COMPLETE when you add the TITHE to your faith. YEAH----THAT'S THE TICKET!! Faith carries us just so far------- but the LAW catapults us to the FINISH LINE". Such a deal!

But the pastor has taken us to the Seventh Chapter of Hebrews, and proven conclusively that Abraham TITHED to Melchezedek, and Abraham lived PRIOR TO the law, and Melchedzedek was a type and foreshadow of Christ. Doesn't this place God's seal of approval to this matter? Well, let's see what the message of Hebrew's Seven is all about.

Hebrews 7

7:1 For this Melchezedek, king of Salem, priest of the most high God, who met Abraham returning from the slaughter of the kings, and blessed him;

2 To whom also Abraham gave a tenth part of all; first being by interpretation King of righteousness, and after that also King of Salem, which is, King of peace;

3 Without father, without mother, without descent, having neither beginning of days, nor end of life; but made like unto the Son of God; abideth a priest continually.

4 Now consider how great this man was, unto whom even the patriarch Abraham gave **the tenth of the spoils.**

5 And verily they that are of the sons of Levi, who receive the office of the priesthood, have a commandment to take tithes of the people **according to the law,** that is, of their brethren, though they come out of the loins of Abraham:

6 But he whose descent is not counted from them **received tithes of Abraham, and blessed him that had the promises.**

7 And without all contradiction the less is blessed of the better.

8 And here men that die receive tithes; but there he receiveth them, of whom it is witnessed that he liveth.

9 And as I may so say, Levi also, who receiveth tithes, payed tithes in Abraham.

10 For he was yet in the loins of his father, when Melchezedek met him.

11 If therefore perfection were by the Levitical priesthood, (for under it the people received the law,) what further need was there that another priest should rise after the order of Melchezedek, and not be called after the order of Aaron?

12 For the priesthood being changed, there is made of necessity a change also of the law.

13 For he of whom these things are spoken pertaineth to another tribe, of which no man gave attendance at the altar.

14 For it is evident that our Lord sprang out of Juda; of which tribe Moses spake nothing concerning priesthood.

15 And it is yet far more evident: for that after the similitude of Melchezedek there ariseth another priest,

16 Who is made, not after the law of a carnal commandment, but after the power of an endless life.

17 For he testifieth, Thou art a priest for ever after the order of Melchezedek.

18 For there is verily a disannulling of the commandment going before for the weakness and unprofitableness thereof.

19 For the law made nothing perfect, but the bringing in of a better hope did; by the which we draw nigh unto God.

20 And inasmuch as not without an oath he was made priest:

21(For those priests were made without an oath; but this with an oath by him that said unto him, The Lord sware and will not repent, Thou art a priest for ever after the order of Melchezedek:)

22 By so much was Jesus made a surety of a better testament.

23 And they truly were many priests, because they were not suffered to continue by reason of death:

24 But this man, because he continueth ever, hath an unchangeable priesthood.

25 Wherefore he is able also to save them to the uttermost that come unto God by him, seeing he ever liveth to make intercession for them.

26 For such an high priest became us, who is holy, harmless, undefiled, separate from sinners, and made higher than the heavens;

27 Who needeth not daily, as those high priests, to offer up sacrifice, first for his own sins, and then for the people's: **for this he did once, when he offered up himself.**

*28 For the law maketh men high priests which have infirmity;
but the word of the oath, which was since the law, maketh
the Son, who is consecrated for evermore.* KJV

To begin with; we are introduced to TWO characters in this
illustration. They are both actual historic characters. They are both
type, and foreshadow of things to come. The first character is an
ancient HIGH PRIEST. He rules from a place called Salem [meaning
"peace"]. Salem is located at a high location [later to be called
Jerusalem]. This man's name is *Melchedzedek.* He is a portrait in
type of *Christ our HIGH PRIEST.*

The second character is Abraham. He is our portrait type of
MANKIND. He precedes the Law and Moses in history. Now the
story begins; Abraham has just returned from a battle in which
he slaughtered several local kings. He has rescued his nephew
LOT, who had been captured by those kings. Abraham also comes
with all the people that had been taken with Lot, and all the
BOOTY OF WAR. This Melchedzedek descends from his throne in
Salem, and meets Abraham in the plains below. Abraham knows
that the KING OF SALEM has come to extract a gift [tithe], and
Abraham respectfully complies. Now HERE is where the whole
thing brings CLARITY to this matter of the TITHE. Abraham gives
TITHE of the booty of war. In exchange; the KING OF SALEM [King
of PEACE], gives BREAD AND WINE to Abraham. Can you see what
has happened here? Abraham gives TITHE ------the representation
of THE LAW; and Melchedzedek gives to ABRAHAM--------BREAD
AND WINE, the very SYMBOL of the New Testament in Christ's
BODY AND BLOOD. This entire story is a portrait of the exchange
made at the cross. It was the exchange of the system of LAW--
-----for that of GRACE. The story goes on to say; "and the LESS
[Abraham] was blessed of the GREATER" [the King of Salem]--
[verse 7]. Do you see in this typology, that GRACE is more excellent
than LAW, and that Melchedzedek [Christ] left his home in Salem
[heaven], and descended to the plain below [earth], and met with
Abraham [mankind], and received the TITHE [law] unto himself,
and blessed Abraham with BREAD AND WINE [the testament in
Christ's body, and blood]------and Abraham [the lesser---the law]

received of Melchedzedek [the greater----the New Covenant in grace]? This is the message of the ENTIRE BOOK OF HEBREWS. The writer WARNS the Hebrew Church to SHUN THE LAW, for in returning to the things of the LAW, one presents himself EXEMPT from the benefits of GRACE-----and there IS NO REMEDY to those who would try to BLEND law and grace.

Heb 6:4-6 For it is impossible for those who were once enlightened, and have tasted of the heavenly gift, and were made partakers of the Holy Ghost,

5 And have tasted the good word of God, and the powers of the world to come,

6 If they shall fall away, to renew them again unto repentance; seeing they crucify to themselves the Son of God afresh, and put him to an open shame

When CHRIST OUR PASSOVER uttered these words: "IT IS FINISHED"; the Temple VEIL that separated God and man, was FOREVER destroyed. Three and one half years into Christ's ministry-------HE CONFIRMED THE [Abrahamic] COVENANT WITH MANY, AND CAUSED THE SACRIFICE AND OBLATION FOR SIN TO CEASE. There is NO LONGER a path to God's blessing, other than that *TRAIL OF BLOOD that flows from the STAUROS.* I beseech you as siblings in Christ, to cease and desist from the coercion in the tithe. It is reprehensible that you should believe that the TITHE survived the cross. Christ PAID THE TITHE for the entirety of human kind. Now our offerings are made in the NEW Holy of Holies---------the heart of God's elect. Our gifts, and giving are far SUPERIOR to that gift given by Abraham. Our gifts are motivated in purity, and recompensed in JOY. FORSAKE THE TITHE, and FORSAKE RELIGIOUS COERCION. If for no other reason----because in your heart, you know it does not work and it is NOT right!

You need not fear curses and poverty by shunning the LAW OF THE TITHE. God is not looking to punish anyone because they do not tithe, nor is he obligated to bless anyone who tithes of necessity----the law. I will always tell anyone who questions my flight from tithing---"if I was still a tither, THEN I would be

----robbing God". My yearly giving far exceeds any amount of tithe that I ever gave when I was in bondage to this Church heresy. Money cannot purchase God's favor. It cannot be argued with any level of honesty, that "tithing" is SUPERIOR to "giving" under the inspiration of the Holy Spirit, for the Holy Spirit is never selfish or stingy. The day that you depart from the tithe is the day that God will begin to bless you to "give abundantly". Your Spirit will find freedom and "giving" will become a delight.

MY MOM

I never thought a thing of it as I was growing up. My mother was a GIVER. She was always digging to the BOTTOM of her purse and scraping the bottom for change. Looking for that extra little TIP, or giving to a beggar. She ALWAYS had something to give in the Church. She ALWAYS FELT that there were people far less fortunate than we, though we were very poor. She worked her youth, and her health away in a garment sweat-shop in the Forties, and Fifties. She worked like a dog, and destroyed her health in the process-----and still believed that OTHERS were needier than she. I never realized it until I was of a VERY mature age----- "Giving" was not an OBLIGATION to her. It was an OPORTUNITY! This was her chance to HELP someone. This woman raised FOUR FAMILIEs on her own. NO MAN to drag her down. Day in, and day out she labored to feed her families. A thought of "THANKS"? NEVER!---
-----FOR WHAT?------DOING WHAT IS RIGHT?--------PLEASE! This GIFT she passed on to me. I am not POORER for it!

CHAPTER VIII

HERESIES AND HERETICS

The encroachment of modern heresy in the Church of the past thirty years began in the "Charismatic Movement" from the 1970s. The Church began to drift from the teaching of sound doctrine into the obsession for miracles and dynamic "praise and worship". As the movement grew, so also the spread of extra-biblical "revelation". "New revelation", was not always "contrary" to scripture, but simply NOT FOUND in scripture thereby causing it to be difficult to rebut. As the movement spread and began to drift in different directions, so also, more erroneous doctrine. In the past twenty years, the trend has leaped forward into downright HERESY, even to the point of denying that the Blood of Christ alone is sufficient to save. They have created for themselves, and those who follow them, a hodge podge mixture of truth and serious heresy. When confronted by orthodox theologians, they simply retreat into orthodoxy until the heat is off, then return to the most heretical doctrines of the Christian age. Many times they walk a thin line between truth and heresy so as NOT TO DRAW FIRE from those who are authoritatively able to confront them. It's a cagy game they play. Unfortunately, for the modern day heretics, they have been recorded and in many cases have been filmed in their folly. They have come to spread their heresies around the world, especially into Africa where there is a willing audience due to the common practice of Witchcraft in the African Church, and extreme poverty. It's an easy transition from Witchcraft into heretical Christianity----especially into the "Prosperity Gospel". As a missionary to Africa, I can tell you that "orthodoxy" has been ravaged in Africa, from Nigeria to Kenya---from South Africa to the Mediterranean it is so. We'll take a look at some American heresies and the heretics that promote them.

Trinity Broadcasting Network is the largest religious broadcasting system in the world. It is also FIRTILE GROUND for the growth of rank heresies. You will, no doubt, recognize many of the TBN heretics named in this book.

Benny Hinn [the 9 persons of the Godhead]

· **Hinn** "Man, I feel revelation knowledge already coming on me here. Life your hands. Something new is going to happen here today. I felt it just as I walked down here. **Holy Spirit, take over in the name of Jesus**...God the Father, ladies and gentlemen, is a person; **and He is a triune being by Himself separate from the Son and the Holy Ghost.** Say, what did you say? Hear it, hear it, hear it. See, God the Father is a person, God the Son is a person, God the Holy Ghost is a person. **But each one of them is a triune being by Himself.** If I can shock you—and maybe I should—**there's nine of them.** Huh, what did you say? Let me explain: **God the Father, ladies and gentlemen, is a person with his own personal spirit, with his own personal soul, and his own personal spirit-body.** You say, Huh, I never heard that. Well you think you're in this church to hear things you've heard for the last 50 years?" (Benny Hinn, Benny Hinn program on TBN (October 3, 1991).

> ❖ SO now the ancient doctrine of the triune Godhead has been replaced with this strange notion of "nine persons of the Godhead?

· **Benny Hinn**

"God came from heaven, became a man, **made man into little gods,** went back to heaven as a man. **He faces the Father as a man. I face**

devils as the son of God. Quit your nonsense! What else are you? If you say, I am, you're saying I'm a part of Him, right? Is he God? Are you His offspring? **Are you His children? You can't be human! You can't! You can't!** God didn't give birth to flesh...You said, "Well, that's heresy." No, that's your crazy brain saying that." (Benny Hinn, Our Position in Christ #2—The Word Made Flesh (Orlando: Orlando Christian Center, 1991), videotape #255.

> ❖ **SO Jesus is a man at the right hand of the Father, and Benny Hinn is God in the earth?**

· **Benny Hinn**

"And let me add this: **Had the Holy Spirit not been with Jesus, He would have sinned.** That's right, it was the Holy Spirit that was the power that kept Him pure. He was not only sent from heaven, but He was called the Son of Man—**and as such He was capable of sinning...** Without the Holy Ghost, Jesus would have never have made it... **Can you imagine Christ headed for the grave, knowing He would remain there forever, if the Holy Ghost would change His mind about raising Him from the dead?**" (Benny Hinn, Good Morning, Holy Spirit (Nashville: Thomas Nelson, 1990), 135-36.

> ❖ **So, Jesus is not eternally and inherently God, even though he was conceived of the Holy Ghost in his mother's womb? So, the Father sent his son on a risky mission into earth trusting that his son would make the right decision and NOT SIN----thereby making the plan of redemption a coin toss?**

· **Benny Hinn**

"Ladies and gentlemen, the serpent is a symbol of Satan. **Jesus Christ knew the only way He would stop Satan is by becoming one in nature with him.** You say, 'What did you say? What blasphemy is this?' No, you hear this! **He did not take my sin; He became my sin.** Sin is the nature of hell. Sin is what made Satan. It was sin that made

Satan. **Jesus said, "I'll be sin! I'll go to the lowest place! I'll go to the origin of it! I won't just take part in it, I'll be the totality of it!" When Jesus became sin, sir, He took it from A to Z and said, "No more!"** Think about this: He became flesh, that flesh might become like Him. He became death, so dying man can live. He became sin, so sinners can be righteous in Him. **He became one with the nature of Satan, so all those who had the nature of Satan can partake of the nature of God."** (Benny Hinn, Benny Hinn program on TBN (December 15, 1990).

❖ **So, in the NATURE OF SATAN Jesus proclaimed ; "Father forgive them, they know not what they do"? and in the NATURE OF SATAN Jesus said to the thief next to him----"Today you will be with me in Paradise"? So, in the NATURE OF SATAN Jesus said "Son. behold thy mother, and mother behold thy son"? So, in the NATURE OF SATAN Jesus said----"Father, into thy hands I commit my Spirit"? So, in the nature of Satan, Jesus uttered "it is finished"? So, in the NATURE OF SATAN, the Spirit of Jesus descended into the lower parts and preached to those who lived before the flood?**

To believe this rot is a show of willful rebellion to God's Holy Word. It shows a willingness on the part of "Word of Faith" followers to usurp themselves above the doctrine of the Apostles and the cornerstone of our faith-----Christ himself, and to submit themselves to those things that will drag them into hell along with their W.O.F. Gods. If indeed "they are Gods" their throne will be everlasting and in HELL!

· **Benny Hinn**,

"My, you know, whoosh! The Holy Ghost is just showing me some stuff. I'm getting dizzy! I'm telling you the truth—it's, it's just heavy right now on me...He's [referring to Jesus] in the underworld now. God is in there, the Holy Ghost is in there, and the Bible says He was begotten. **Do you know what the word begotten means? It means reborn.** Do you want another shocker? Have you been begotten?

So was He. Don't let anyone deceive you. **Jesus was reborn. You say, 'What are you talking about?'…He was reborn. He had to be reborn…If He was not reborn, I could not be reborn, I would never be reborn. How can I face Jesus and say, "Jesus, You went through everything I've gone through, except the new birth?"** (Benny Hinn, Our Position 'In Christ]

❖ **So, the sinless Jesus was BORN AGAIN IN HELL?**

BENNY HINN

: "When you say, 'I am a Christian, you are saying, 'I am mashiach' in the Hebrew. I am a little messiah walking on earth, in other words That is a shocking revelation . . . May I say it like this? You are a little god on earth running around." (Benny Hinn Praise-a-thon TBN November 6, 1990) . . .

❖ **So, now I am a LITTLE Messiah and the Messiah of Israel is just a man?**

Benny Hinn

"Christians are "Little Messiah's and "little gods" on the earth. Thus [Encouraging the audience] . . . say "I am a God-man . . . This spirit-man within me is a God-man . . ." say "I'm born of heaven-a God-man. I'm a God man. I am a sample of Jesus. I'm a super being. Say it! Say it! Who's a super being? "I walk in the realm of the supernatural." Say it! . . . You want to prosper? Money will be falling on you from left, right and centre. God will begin to prosper you, for money always follows righteousness . . . Say after me, "everything I ever want is in me already." (Benny Hinn, TBN, 1990) . . .

❖ **Just call me SUPER MAN----or SUPER DAN!**

Benny Hinn

"When you were born again the Word was made flesh in you. **You are everything He was and everything He is and ever He shall be . . .**

Don't say,' I have.' Say, ' I am, I am, I am, I am, I am." (Benny Hinn, "Our Position in Christ #2-The Word Made Flesh" 1991, audiotape #A031190-2, side 2.)

❖ **Can't wait to WALK ON WATER.**

The FAILED PROPHESIES OF BENNY HINN

April 2nd, 2000 - TBN Praise-a-thon

Benny Hinn" Ladies and gentleman, *Jesus is shaking the world!* Now something else is happening that is to me *awesome! Absolutely awesome!* The Lord is *physically* appearing in the Muslim world. I'm telling you, Paul, I am hearing it now more and more and more. Since we preachers cannot go there, Jesus is - just going there Himself. Since we preachers are not *permitted* to go in, He is just showing up - Himself. You know the Scriptures says clearly that the Lord *did* appear, did He not? Ah for forty days, isn't that right? And the, and the, and the Scriptures says he, he, he even, he even appeared to Paul. Now we are always thinking, well Jesus can't really preach, preach the Gospel. Who told you that? He was the first one *to* preach the Gospel. In fact He is the one who came to Paul and said, *Paul, I am Jesus.* He, He didn't send no angel to do that job. He did it Himself. If Jesus revealed Himself to Paul, why not reveal Himself to a lot more than just Paul? *And He is doing it!* The reason the Lord had to appear to Paul is because He knew Paul wouldn't listen to nobody else. Now in the case of Cornelius, the angel said send for Peter, 'cause, because Cornelius was, was ready, his heart was right, he'd been in prayer. But here's Paul killing everybody, causing 'em to blaspheme, Jesus said this man won't even listen to an angel, so I'll go do the job myself. So He went and knocked him right off his horse and preached the Gospel to him. **He's doing the same thing today in the Muslim world. He's appearing, *hear this*, He is appearing to *Muslims,* saying I am Jesus of Nazareth! And they're coming to know the Lord!** Why are those things happening? It's the last days! Saints, this is why we need to give to the Gospel *now* more than ever. You know naively say well I gave last year. Forget it! Last year it's gone! That cycle is over with! Seed time - harvest of last year is gone. Every season is a fresh season. We are in a *fresh* season. What, what you gave last year will not reap you anything this year. What you gave even a few months ago is *gone*, you *got* the harvest for that."

April 2nd, 2000 - TBN Praise-a-thon

Benny Hinn "The hour is *urgent*. Many of you have known me for many years. But I am telling you right now, things I haven't said years 'n years 'n years ago. I believe - *here this, hear this!* **I believe, that Jesus, God's Son, is about to appear *physically*, in meetings and to believers around the world, to *wake us up!* He appeared *after* His resurrection and He is about to appear *before* His second coming!** You know a prophetess sent me a word through my wife, right here, and she said 'Tell your husband that Jesus is go'n to *physically* appear in his meetings.' I am expecting to see, I am telling you that - I feel it's going to happen. I, I, I'm, I'm careful in how I am saying it now, because I know the people in Kenya are listening. I know deep in my soul, something *supernatural* is going to happen in Nai - in Nairobi Kenya.** I *feel* that. I may very well come back, and you and Jan are coming, to - Paul and Jan are coming to Nairobi with me, but Paul, **we may very well come back with footage of Jesus on the platform! You know that the Lord appeared in Romania recently, and there's a video of it? Where the Lord appeared in the back of a church and you see him on video walking down the isle?** Yeah! Paul do you remember when I came on TBN years ago and showed you a clip of the Lord appearing in our church in Orlando, on the balcony on the wall? Yeah. You, you remember that? [Paul Crouch] Very well, I saw it! [Benny Hinn] That was '80, 80 something, '86, what - whatever. You know I always wondered why the Lord, why did He do that? Do you know why, now I look back? That was the beginning of the greatest move of God in our church. Because '83, '84, and '85 were horrible years for me, horrible years. Eighty-six the blessings of God began, but they began with a - with this manifestation of the Lord's face on, on the balcony, that stayed for eight weeks. *Eight solid weeks!* The Lord has done this in the past, but He is about to do it again, now hear this, *I am prophesying this!* Jesus Christ, the Son of God, is about to appear *physically* in some churches, and some meetings, and to many of His people, for one reason - to tell you He is about to show up! To Wake Up! Jesus is coming saints! You have held back from the Lord in the past, don't you *dare* do it now. The day will come you'll stand before Him and give an answer. How *dare* we not give to God. How *dare* we hold back."

April 21st, 2000 - This Is Your Day

Benny Hinn "You know, yesterday on the program I was telling you and the audience here that Ruth Heflin, the prophetess, had sent me a word from the Lord, where she said that the Lord had spoken to her clearly, that, a, for me to prepare myself, for the Lord is going to *visibly appear, on the platform*, in one of our crusades. I pray it'll happen in every crusade. But I have a feeling, I am just telling you honestly, I have even told some of our staff, when I go to Kenya, I am going to Kenya in just a few days from now, a *million* people will be in Kenya, Nairobi. I feel *in my being* it is going to happen there. **So pray for us as we go to Kenya. I pray it will happen *tonight*, at the good Friday service in Nashville. I pray it will happen in *every* crusade.**"

❖   **IT NEVER HAPPENED----EVER!**

Creflo Dollar

Here's what I want you to get here. **If Jesus came as God, then why did God have to anoint Him?** If Jesus - see God's already been anointed. If Jesus came as God, then why did God have to anoint Him? **Jesus came as a man, that's why it was legal to anoint him. God doesn't need anointing**, He is anointing. Jesus came as a man, and at age 30 God is now getting ready to demonstrate to us, **and give us an example of what a man, with the anointing, can do.**
-- Creflo Dollar

Jesus didn't come as God, he came as a man, and he did not come perfect. Perfect in the sense that he didn't need to be added to.
-- Creflo Dollar

But Jesus didn't show up perfect, he grew into his perfection. You know Jesus, in one scripture in the Bible he went on a journey, and he was tired. You better hope God don't get tired. Isaiah 50 says, 50, 60, somewhere, says where we have a God who fainteth not, neither is weary (Isa. 40:28). But Jesus did, if he came as God and he got tired, he says he sat down by the well 'cause he was tired. Boy we're in trouble. And somebody said, well, Jesus came as God. Well how many of **you know the Bible says God never sleeps, nor slumbers. And yet in the book of Mark we see Jesus asleep in the back of the boat.** Y'all please listen to me, please listen to me. This ain't no heresy. I am not some false prophet, I am just reading this thing out to you the Bible. I am just telling you all these fantasy preachers have been preaching all of this stuff for all of these years and we bought the package. And the question mark was there. And we are now - faith can never go past that question mark, and we've tolerated and put it up, put up with things that we had authority over . . . -- Creflo Dollar

❖ **The Bible is clear on this issue. Jesus is/was inherently and eternally----GOD!**

1 Tim 3:16

And without controversy great is the mystery of godliness: **God was manifest in the flesh,** *justified in the Spirit, seen of angels, preached unto the Gentiles, believed on in the world, received up into glory.*

John 1:1-5

1:1 In the beginning was the Word, **and the Word was with God, and the Word was God.** *2 He was with God in the beginning.*

3 Through him all things were made; **without him nothing was made that has been made.** *4 In him was life, and that life was the*

light of men. 5 The light shines in the darkness, but the darkness has not understood it. NIV

John 20:26-29

26 A week later his disciples were in the house again, and Thomas was with them. Though the doors were locked, Jesus came and stood among them and said, "Peace be with you!"

27 Then he said to Thomas, "Put your finger here; see my hands. Reach out your hand and put it into my side. Stop doubting and believe."

28 Thomas said to him, "**My Lord and my God!**" NIV

John 1:15-18

15 John testifies concerning him. He cries out, saying, "This was he of whom I said, 'He who comes after me has surpassed me because he was before me.'"

16 From the fullness of his grace we have all received one blessing after another.

17 For the law was given through Moses; grace and truth came through Jesus Christ.

18 No one has ever seen God, but God the One and Only, who is at the Father's side, has made him known.

John 8:58-59

58 "I tell you the truth," Jesus answered**, "before Abraham was born, I am!"** 59 At this, they picked up stones to stone him, but Jesus hid himself, slipping away from the temple grounds. NIV

Heb 1:8-13

8 But about the Son he says,

"Your throne, O God, will last forever and ever,

and righteousness will be the scepter of your kingdom.

9 You have loved righteousness and hated wickedness;

*therefore God, your God, **has set you above your companions***

by anointing you with the oil of joy."

10 He also says,

*"**In the beginning, O Lord, you laid the foundations of the earth,***

and the heavens are the work of your hands.

11 They will perish, but you remain;

they will all wear out like a garment.

12 You will roll them up like a robe;

like a garment they will be changed.

But you remain the same,

and your years will never end."

13 To which of the angels did God ever say,

"Sit at my right hand

until I make your enemies

a footstool for your feet"? NIV

<u>*Heb 1:10-13*</u>

10 He also says,

*"**In the beginning, O Lord, you laid the foundations of the earth,***

and the heavens are the work of your hands.

11 They will perish, but you remain;

they will all wear out like a garment.

12 You will roll them up like a robe;

like a garment they will be changed.

But you remain the same,

and your years will never end."

13 To which of the angels did God ever say,

"Sit at my right hand

until I make your enemies

a footstool for your feet"? NIV

<u>Col 2:8-10</u>

8 See to it that no one takes you captive through hollow and deceptive philosophy, which depends on human tradition and the basic principles of this world rather than on Christ.

*9 For in Christ all **the fullness of the Deity lives in bodily form,** 10 and you have been given fullness in Christ, who is the head over every power and authority.NIV*

<u>Col 1:15-20</u>

*15 **He is the image of the invisible God**, the firstborn over all creation.*

*16 **For by him all things were created: things in heaven and on earth, visible and invisible,** whether thrones or powers or rulers or authorities; all things were created by him and for him.*

*17 **He is before all things, and in him all things hold together.***

18 And he is the head of the body, the church; he is the beginning and the firstborn from among the dead, so that in everything he might have the supremacy.

*19 **For God was pleased to have all his fullness dwell in him,***

20 and through him to reconcile to himself all things, whether things on earth or things in heaven, by making peace through his blood, shed on the cross. NIV

<u>Matt 1:22-23</u>

22 Now all this was done, that it might be fulfilled which was spoken of the Lord by the prophet, saying,

23 Behold, a virgin shall be with child, and shall bring forth a son, and they shall call his name Emmanuel, which being interpreted is, **God with us.** KJV

<u>1 Tim 3:16</u>

And without controversy great is the mystery of godliness: **God was manifest in the flesh,** justified in the Spirit, seen of angels, preached unto the Gentiles, believed on in the world, received up into glory.

· Kenneth Copeland,

"I was shocked when I found out who the biggest failure in the Bible actually is...The biggest one in the whole Bible is God...Now, the reason you don't think of God as a failure is He never said He's a failure. And you're not a failure till you say you're one." (Kenneth Copeland, Praise-a-Thon program on TBN (April 1988). He also said, **"Adam committed high treason; and at that point, all the dominion and authority God had given to him was handed over to Satan. Suddenly, God was on the outside looking in**...After Adam's fall, God found Himself in a peculiar position...God needed an avenue back into the earth...God laid out His proposition and Abram accepted it. It gave God access to the earth and gave man access to God..**Technically, if God ever broke the Covenant, He would have to destroy Himself."** (Kenneth Copeland, Our Covenant with God (Fort Worth, TX: KCP Publications, 1987), 8-11 passim.

· **Kenneth Copeland:**

"**God's on the outside looking in. He doesn't have any legal entree into the earth.** The thing don't belong to Him. You see how sassy the Devil was in the presence of God in the book of Job? God said, Where have you been? Wasn't any of God's business. He [Satan] didn't even have to answer if he didn't want to..God didn't argue with him a bit! You see, this is the position that God's been in...Might say, '**Well, if God's running things He's doing a lousy job of it.**" **He hadn't been running 'em, except when He's just got, you know, a little bit of a chance.**" (Kenneth Copeland, Image of God in You III (Fort Worth, TX: Kenneth Copeland Ministries, 1989), audiotape #01-1403, side 1.

· **Copeland**

"The Bible says that God gave this earth to the sons of men...and when [Adam] turned and gave that dominion to Satan, look where it left God. If left Him on the outside looking in...He had no legal right to do anything about it, did He?...He had injected Himself illegally into the earth—what Satan had intended for Him to do was to fall for it—pull off an illegal act and turn the light off in God, and subordinate God to himself...He intended to get God into such a trap t hat He couldn't get out." (Kenneth Copeland, What Happened from the Cross to the Throne (Fort Worth, TX: Kenneth Copeland Ministries, 1990), audiotape #02-0017..

· **Kenneth Copeland:**

"**[Adam] was the copy, looked just like [God]. If you stood Adam upside God, they look just exactly alike.** If yo stood Jesus and Adam side-by-side, they would look and sound exactly alike." (Kenneth Copeland, Authority of the Believer IV (Fort Worth, TX: Kenneth Copeland Ministries, 1987), audiotape #01-0304, side 1.

· **Copeland**

"Don't be disturbed when people put you down and speak harshly and roughly of you. They spoke that way of Me, should they not speak that way of you? The more you get to be like Me, the more they're going to think that way of you. **They crucified Me for claiming that I was God. But I didn't claim I was God**; I just claimed I walked with Him and that He was in Me. Hallelujah." (Kenneth Copeland, Take Time to Pray, Believer's Voice of Victory 15, 2 (February 1987): 9.

· Copeland

"What [why] does God have to pay the price for this thing? He has to have a man that is like that first one. It's got to be a man. **He's got to be all man. He cannot be a God** and come storming in here will attributes and dignities that are not common to man. He can't do that. It's not legal." (Kenneth Copeland, What Happened from the Cross to the Throne (Fort Worth, TX: Kenneth Copeland Ministries, 1990), audiotape #02-0017.

· Copeland

"Here's where we're gonna depart from ordinary church: Now, you see, God is injecting His Word into the earth to produce this Jesus—these faith-filled words that framed the image that's in Him... **He can't just walk onto the earth and say, "Let it be!" because He doesn't have the right. He had to sneak it in here around the god of this world that was blockin' every way that he possibly could."** (Kenneth Copeland, The Image of God in You III (Fort Worth, TX: Kenneth Copeland Ministries, 1989), audiotape #01-1403, side , **"God was making promises to Jesus, and Jesus wasn't even there. But, you see, God deals with things that are not yet as though they already were. That's the way He gets them to come to pass."** (Kenneth Copeland, What Happened from the Cross to the Throne (Fort Worth, TX: Kenneth Copeland Ministries, 1990), audiotape #02-0017.

· Copeland

"The righteousness of God was made to be sin. **He accepted the sin nature of Satan in His own spirit.** And at the moment that He did so, He cried, "My God, My God, why hast thou forsaken Me?" You don't know what happened at the cross. Why do you think Moses, upon instruction of God, raised the serpent upon that pole instead of a lamb? That used to bug me. I said, "Why in the world would you want to put a snake up there—the sign of Satan? Why didn't you put a lamb on that pole?" And the Lord said, "Because it was a sign of Satan that was hanging on the cross." **He said, "I accepted, in My own spirit, spiritual death; and the light was turned off."** (Kenneth Copeland, What Happened from the Cross to the Throne (Fort Worth, TX: Kenneth Copeland Ministries, 1990), audiotape #02-0017, side 2.

> ❖ May I say---Jesus is the light of the world, and his light shines in darkness, and darkness cannot dispel it. That LIGHT is ETERNAL and cannot be extinguished!

John 1

1:1 In the beginning was the Word, and the Word was with God, and the Word was God.

2 The same was in the beginning with God.

3 All things were made by him; and without him was not anything made that was made.

*4 In him was life; **and the life was the light of men***

*5 **And the light shineth in darkness; and the darkness comprehended it not.***

> ❖ What BLASPHEMY these heretics speak.

Kenneth Hagin

also claims that **Jesus Christ took on the nature of Satan,** "spiritual death means something more than separation from God. Spiritual death also means having Satan's nature...Jesus tasted death—spiritual death—for every man." (Kenneth E. Hagin, The Name of Jesus (Tulsa, OK: Kenneth Hagin Ministries, 1981), 31.

> ❖ These are the words of Jesus as he departed from this life into eternity------"Father, into thy hands I commit my Spirit". Are these the words of a man who has taken on the

Nature of Satan? If heresy could be numbered one to ten in its level of offence, this heresy would a resounding---- eleven.

· **Kenneth Hagin**

"Man...was created on terms of equality with God, and **he could stand in God's presence without any consciousness of inferiority... God has made us as much like Himself as possible...He made us the same class of being that He is Himself**...Man lived in the realm of God. He lived on terms equal with God...The believer is called Christ...That's who we are; we're Christ!" (Kenneth M. Hagin, Zoe: The God-Kind of Life (Tulsa, OK: Kenneth Hagin Ministries, Inc., 1989), 35-36, 41.

· **Kenneth Copeland**

"God's reason for creating Adam was His desire to reproduce Himself...He was not a little like God. He was not almost like God. He was not subordinate to God even." (Kenneth Copeland, Following the Faith of Abraham I (Fort Worth, TX: Kenneth Copeland Ministries, 1989), tape #01-3001, side 1.

❖ **Like his student [Kenneth Copeland], Hagin teaches that Adam was in no way subordinate or inferior to God. This is what the Bible has to say about the matter.**

Gen 2:15-17

*15 The LORD God **took the man and put him in the Garden of Eden to work it and take care of it. 16 And the LORD God commanded the man, "You are free to eat from any tree in the garden;***

17 but you must not eat from the tree of the knowledge of good and evil, for when you eat of it you will surely die."

Heresy-----Insufficiency of the CROSS

· **Kenneth Hagin**

"He [Jesus] tasted spiritual death for every man. And His spirit and inner man went to hell in my place. Can't you see that? Physical death wouldn't remove your sins. He's tasted death for every man. He's talking about tasting spiritual death." (Kenneth E. Hagin, How Jesus Obtained His Name (Tulsa, OK: Kenneth Hagin Ministries, n.d.), tape #44H01, side 1.

Fredrick K.C. Price

Frederick Price:

"Do you think that the punishment for our sin was to die on a cross? If that were the case, the two thieves could have paid your price. No, the punishment was to go into hell itself and to serve time in hell separated from God...Satan and all the demons of hell thought that they had Him bound and they threw a net over Jesus and dragged Him down to the very pit of hell itself to serve our sentence." (Frederick K.C. Price, Ever Increasing Faith Messanger (June 1980),

JOYCE MEYER

"Whatever it took to get God's people back, free again, is what they would do. Jesus paid for our sins on the cross **and went to hell in our place."** (The Most Important Decision You Will Ever Make Page 41, 1996-Edition)

"There is no hope of anyone going to heaven unless they believe this truth I am presenting. You cannot go to heaven unless you believe with all your heart that Jesus took your place in hell" (1991 booklet, *The Most Important Decision You Will Ever Make*).

❖ Like so many other W.O.F [Word of Faith] preachers, Meyers has bought into the "redemption in hell" doctrine. She goes so far as to contend that one "cannot be saved unless one believes that his/her redemption was purchased in hell".

Meyer--- **"During that time He entered hell,** where you and I deserved to go (legally) because of our sin. He paid the price there . . . no plan was too extreme . . . Jesus paid <u>on the cross and in hell</u>" (*The Most Important Decision You Will Ever Make* 1991 p. 35,). **"He went to hell to pay the debt you owed".** (p.41 first edition)

· **Kenneth Copeland**

"When Jesus cried, 'It is finished!' **He was not speaking of the plan of redemption.** There were still three days and nights to go through before He went to the throne...**Jesus' death on the cross was only the beginning of the complete work of redemption.**" (Kenneth Copeland, Jesus—Our Lord of Glory, Believer's Voice of Victory 10, 4 (April 1982):3.

❖   **Well, let's just trash this heresy real quick.**

THE BLOOD

John 6:53-57

53 Then Jesus said unto them, Verily, verily, I say unto you, Except ye eat the flesh of the Son of man, and drink his blood, ye have no life in you.

*54 **Whoso eateth my flesh, and drinketh my blood**, hath eternal life; and I will raise him up at the last day.*

55 For my flesh is meat indeed, and my blood is drink indeed.

56 He that eateth my flesh, and drinketh my blood, dwelleth in me, and I in him.

Rom 3:25-26

*25 Whom God hath set forth to be **a propitiation through faith in his blood**, to declare his righteousness for the remission of sins that are past, through the forbearance of God;*

26 To declare, I say, at this time his righteousness: that he might be just, and the justifier of him which believeth in Jesus KJV

<u>Rom 5:9-11</u>

*9 Much more then, **being now justified by his blood,** we shall be saved from wrath through him.*

*10 For if, when we were enemies, we were reconciled to God **by the death of his Son,** much more, being reconciled, we shall be saved by his life. KJV*

<u>1 Cor 11:25-29</u>

*25 After the same manner also he took the cup, when he had supped, **saying, This cup is the new testament in my blood:** this do ye, as oft as ye drink it, in remembrance of me.*

26 For as often as ye eat this bread, and drink this cup, ye do shew the Lord's death till he come.

27 Wherefore whosoever shall eat this bread, and drink this cup of the Lord, unworthily, shall be guilty of the body and blood of the Lord.

28 But let a man examine himself, and so let him eat of that bread, and drink of that cup. KJV

<u>Eph 1:7</u>

***7 In whom we have redemption through his blood,** the forgiveness of sins, according to the riches of his grace;*

<u>Eph 2:13</u>

*13 But now in Christ Jesus ye who sometimes were far off **are made nigh by the blood of Christ.** KJV*

<u>Col 1:14-21</u>

***14 In whom we have redemption through his blood,** even the forgiveness of sins:*

15 Who is the image of the invisible God, the firstborn of every creature:

16 **For by him were all things created, that are in heaven, and that are in earth,** visible and invisible, whether they be thrones, or dominions, or principalities, or powers: all things were created by him, and for him:

17 And he is before all things, and by him all things consist.

18 And he is the head of the body, the church: who is the beginning, the firstborn from the dead; that in all things he might have the preeminence.

19 For it pleased the Father that in him should all fulness dwell;

20 And, **having made peace through the blood of his cross**, by him to reconcile all things unto himself; by him, I say, whether they be things in earth, or things in heaven. KJV

Heb 9:12-15

12 Neither by the blood of goats and calves, **but by his own blood he entered in once into the holy place,** having obtained eternal redemption for us.

13 For if the blood of bulls and of goats, and the ashes of an heifer sprinkling the unclean, sanctifieth to the purifying of the flesh:

14 **How much more shall the blood of Christ**, who through the eternal Spirit offered himself without spot to God, **purge your conscience** from dead works to serve the living God? KJV

Heb 10:19-23

19 Having therefore, brethren, boldness to enter into the holiest **by the blood of Jesus,**

20 By a new and living way, **which he hath consecrated for us**, through the veil, that is to say, **his flesh;**

21 And having an high priest over the house of God;

22 Let us draw near with a true heart in full assurance of faith, having our hearts sprinkled from an evil conscience, and our bodies washed with pure water.

Heb 12:24-25

*24 And to Jesus the mediator of the new covenant, **and to the blood of sprinkling**, that speaketh better things than that of Abel. KJV*

Heb 13:12-13

12 Wherefore Jesus also, that he might sanctify the people with his own blood, suffered without the gate.

I Pet.1:2

*2 Elect according to the foreknowledge of God the Father, through sanctification of the Spirit, unto obedience **and sprinkling of the blood of Jesus Christ**: Grace unto you, and peace, be multiplied.*

Rev 1:5-6

*5 And from Jesus Christ, who is the faithful witness, and the first begotten of the dead, and the prince of the kings of the earth. Unto him that loved us, **and washed us from our sins in his own blood,** KJV*

Rev 5:9-11

*9 And they sung a new song, saying, Thou art worthy to take the book, and to open the seals thereof: for thou wast slain**, and hast redeemed us to God by thy blood** out of every kindred, and tongue, and people, and nation;*

10 And hast made us unto our God kings and priests: and we shall reign on the earth. KJV

Rev 7:14-16

*14 And I said unto him, Sir, thou knowest. And he said to me, These are they which came out of great tribulation, and have washed their robes, **and made them white in the blood of the Lamb.***

15 Therefore are they before the throne of God, and serve him day and night in his temple: and he that sitteth on the throne shall dwell among them. KJV

THE CROSS

Eph.2:15

15 Having abolished in his flesh the enmity, even the law of commandments contained in ordinances; for to make in himself of twain one new man, so making peace;

16 And that he might reconcile **both unto God in one body by the cross**, having slain the enmity thereby:

17 And came and preached peace to you which were afar off, and to them that were nigh.

Col. 1:18

18 And he is the head of the body, the church: who is the beginning, the firstborn from the dead; that in all things he might have the preeminence.

19 For it pleased the Father that in him should all fulness dwell;

20 And, **having made peace through the blood of his cross**, by him to reconcile all things unto himself; by him, I say, whether they be things in earth, or things in heaven. KJV

Col 2:14-15

14 Blotting out the handwriting of ordinances that was against us, which was contrary to us, **and took it out of the way, nailing it to his cross**;

15 And having spoiled principalities and powers, he made a shew of them openly, triumphing over them in it KJV

<u>Heb 12:2-3</u>

*2 Looking unto Jesus the author and finisher of our faith; who for the joy that was set before him **endured the cross**, despising the shame, and is set down at the right hand of the throne of God. KJV*

REDEMPTION

<u>Rom 3:24-26</u>

24 Being justified freely by his grace through the redemption that is in Christ Jesus:

*25 **Whom God hath set forth to be a propitiation through faith in his blood**, to declare his righteousness for the remission of sins that are past, through the forbearance of God; KJV*

<u>Eph 1:7</u>

*7 **In whom we have redemption through his blood**, the forgiveness of sins, according to the riches of his grace; KJV*

<u>Col 1:14-15</u>

*14 **In whom we have redemption through his blood**, even the forgiveness of sins:*

<u>Heb 9:12-15</u>

*12 Neither by the blood of goats and calves, **but by his own blood he entered in once into the holy place, having obtained eternal redemption for us**.*

13 For if the blood of bulls and of goats, and the ashes of an heifer sprinkling the unclean, sanctifieth to the purifying of the flesh:

14 How much more shall the blood of Christ, who through the eternal Spirit offered himself without spot to God, purge your conscience from dead works to serve the living God? KJV

Danny McDowell

Heb 9:12-13

*12 Neither by the blood of goats and calves, but by his own blood he entered in once into the holy place, **having obtained eternal redemption for us.***

❖ When Jesus cried out "it is finished", the veil in the Temple was torn from top to bottom, signifying that the Covenant with Abraham had been CONFIRMED in the Body and Blood of the eternal Passover Lamb. The W.O.F preachers/teachers deny the POWER of the CROSS to save. It is the most serious heresy in the history of the Church.

Heresy-----The Deity of MAN

· **Kenneth Hagin**

"**Man…was created on terms of equality with God, and he could stand in God's presence without any consciousness of inferiority…** God has made us as much like Himself as possible…**He made us the same class of being that He is Himself…Man lived in the realm of God. He lived on terms equal with God**…The believer is called Christ…That's who we are; we're Christ!" (Kenneth M. Hagin, Zoe: The God-Kind of Life (Tulsa, OK: Kenneth Hagin Ministries, Inc., 1989), 35-36, 41.

· **Kenneth Copeland**

"God's reason for creating Adam was His desire to reproduce Himself…He was not a little like God. He was not almost like God. **He was not subordinate to God even.**" (Kenneth Copeland, Following the Faith of Abraham I (Fort Worth, TX: Kenneth Copeland Ministries, 1989), tape #01-3001, side 1.

· **John Avanzini**

The Spirit of God "declared in the earth today what the eternal purpose of God has been through the ages…**that He is duplicating Himself on earth.**" (John Avanzini with Morris Cerullo, The Endtime

Manifestation of the Sons of God, (San Diego: Morris Cerullo World Evangelism, n.d.), audiotape 1, side 2.

· Morris Cerullo

"Did you know that from the beginning of time the whole purpose of God was to reproduce Himself?...Who are you? Come on, who are you? Come on, say it: 'Sons of God!' Come on, say it! And what does work inside us, brother, is that manifestation of the expression of all that God is and all that God has. **And when we stand up here, brother, you're not looking at Morris Cerullo; you're looking at God.** You're looking at Jesus." (Morris Cerullo, The End time Manifestation of the Sons of God, (San Diego: Morris Cerullo World Evangelism, n.d.), audiotape 1, sides1 & 2.

Isa 42:8

8 "I am the LORD; that is my name!

I will not give my glory to another

or my praise to idols. NIV

Isa 43:11-13

11 I, even I, am the LORD,

and apart from me there is no savior.

12 I have revealed and saved and proclaimed--

I, and not some foreign god among you.

You are my witnesses," declares the LORD, "that I am God.

13 Yes, and from ancient days I am he.

No one can deliver out of my hand.

When I act, who can reverse it?" NIV

Isa 45:5

5 I am the LORD, and there is no other;

apart from me there is no God.*NIV*

Isa 45:6-7

I am the LORD, **and there is no other.**

7 I form the light and create darkness,

I bring prosperity and create disaster;

I, the LORD, do all these things. NIV

Isa 45:18-19

8 For this is what the LORD says--

he who created the heavens,

he is God;

he who fashioned and made the earth,

he founded it;

he did not create it to be empty,

but formed it to be inhabited--

he says:

"I am the LORD,

and there is no other.

19 I have not spoken in secret,

from somewhere in a land of darkness;

I have not said to Jacob's descendants,

'Seek me in vain.'

I, the LORD, speak the truth;

I declare what is right. NIV

Jer 32:26-27

*26 Then the word of the LORD came to Jeremiah: 27 "**I am the LORD, the God of all mankind.** Is anything too hard for me? NIV*

Ezek 7:4

*4 I will not look on you with pity or spare you; I will surely repay you for your conduct **and the detestable practices among you.** Then you will know that I am the LORD. NIV*

Ezek 16:62-63

62 So I will establish my covenant with you, and you will know that I am the LORD.

*63 Then, when I make atonement for you for all you have done, you will remember and be ashamed **and never again open your mouth because of your humiliation,** declares the Sovereign LORD.'" NIV*

Heresy------God is a man and Man is God

· Kenneth Copeland

God is a being that is very uncanny the way He's very much like you and me. **A being that stands somewhere around 6'-2", 6'-3", that weighs somewhere in the neighborhood of a couple of hundred pounds, little better, [and] has a [hand] span of nine inches across."** (Kenneth Copeland, Spirit, Soul and Body I (Fort Worth, TX: Kenneth Copeland Ministries, 1985), audiotape #01-0601, side 1.

· Jerry Savelle

He [God] is measured out heaven with a nine-inch span...The distance between my thumb and my finger is not quite nine inches. So, I know He's bigger than me, thank God. Amen? But He's not some great, big, old thing that couldn't come through the door there and, you know, when He sat down, would fill every seat in the house. I don't serve the Glob." (Jerry Savelle, Framing Your World with the Word of God, Part 2 (Fort Worth, TX: Jerry Savelle Evangelistic Association, Inc., n.d.), audiotape #SS-36, side 1.

· Morris Cerullo

"As I lay there on the floor in this condition, my spirit was taken out of my body and the next thing I knew, I was in the heavens... Suddenly, in front of this tremendous multitude of people, the glory of God appeared. **The Form that I saw was about the height of a man six feet tall, maybe a little taller, and twice as broad as a human body with no distinguishing features such as eyes, nose, or mouth."** (Morris Cerullo, The Miracle Book (San Diego, CA: Cerullo Word Evangelism, Inc., 1984), x-xi.

· Benny Hinn,

"I could almost visibly see the Lord, and I could tell you what He was wearing." **Jan Crouch**, giddy about Hinn's statement, asks, "Was that the Holy Spirit?" Acknowledging that he may get in trouble, Hinn resolutely answers "yes." (Benny Hinn and Jan Crouch, Praise the Lord program on TBN (October 3, 1991).

· Kenneth Copeland said

, "I was shocked when I found out who the biggest failure in the Bible actually is...**The biggest one in the whole Bible is God**...Now, the reason you don't think of God as a failure is He never said He's a failure. And you're not a failure till you say you're one." (Kenneth Copeland, Praise-a-Thon program on TBN (April 1988).

-Kenneth Copeland

"Adam committed high treason; and at that point, all the dominion and authority God had given to him was handed over to Satan. Suddenly, God was on the outside looking in...After Adam's fall, God found Himself in a peculiar position...God needed an avenue back into the earth...God laid out His proposition and Abram accepted it. It gave God access to the earth and gave man access to God..Technically, if God ever broke the Covenant, He would have to destroy Himself." (Kenneth Copeland, Our Covenant with God (Fort Worth, TX: KCP Publications, 1987), 8-11 passim.

· **Benny Hinn**

"**God came from heaven, became a man, made man into little gods, went back to heaven as a man. He faces the Father as a man. I face devils as the son of God.**.Quit your nonsense! What else are you? If you say, I am, you're saying I'm a part of Him, right? Is he God? Are you His offspring**? Are you His children? You can't be human!** You can't! You can't! God didn't give birth to flesh...You said, "Well, that's heresy." No, that's your crazy brain saying that." (Benny Hinn, Our Position in Christ #2—The Word Made Flesh (Orlando: Orlando Christian Center, 1991), videotape #255.

· **Kenneth Copeland**:

"God's on the outside looking in. **He doesn't have any legal entree into the earth. The thing don't belong to Him.** You see how sassy the Devil was in the presence of God in the book of Job? God said, Where have you been? **Wasn't any of God's business.** He [Satan] didn't even have to answer if he didn't want to..God didn't argue with him a bit! You see, this is the position that God's been in...**Might say, 'Well, if God's running things He's doing a lousy job of it." He hadn't been running 'em, except when He's just got, you know, a little bit of a chance.**" (Kenneth Copeland, Image of God in You III (Fort Worth, TX: Kenneth Copeland Ministries, 1989), audiotape #01-1403, side 1.

· **Copeland**

"The Bible says that God gave this earth to the sons of men...and when [Adam] turned and gave that dominion to Satan, **look where it left God. If left Him on the outside looking in...He had no legal right to do anything about it, did He?**...He had injected Himself illegally into the earth—**what Satan had intended for Him to do was to fall for it—pull off an illegal act and turn the light off in God, and subordinate God to himself...He intended to get God into such a trap that He couldn't get out.**" (Kenneth Copeland, What Happened from the Cross to the Throne (Fort Worth, TX: Kenneth Copeland Ministries, 1990), audiotape #02-0017.

· **Kenneth Copeland:**

"[Adam] was the copy, looked just like [God]. **If you stood Adam upside God, they look just exactly alike.** If yoo stood Jesus and Adam side-by-side, they would look and sound exactly alike." (Kenneth Copeland, Authority of the Believer IV (Fort Worth, TX: Kenneth Copeland Ministries, 1987), audiotape #01-0304, side 1.

· **Kenneth Copeland**

"Don't be disturbed when people put you down and speak harshly and roughly of you. They spoke that way of Me [Jesus], should they not speak that way of you? The more you get to be like Me, the more they're going to think that way of you. **They crucified Me for claiming that I was God. But I didn't claim I was God; I** just claimed I walked with Him and that He was in Me. Hallelujah." (Kenneth Copeland, Take Time to Pray, Believer's Voice of Victory 15, 2 (February 1987): 9.

· **Copeland**

"What [why] does God have to pay the price for this thing? He has to have a man that is like that first one. **It's got to be a man. He's got to be all man.** He cannot be a God and come storming in here will attributes and dignities that are not common to man. He can't do that. It's not legal." (Kenneth Copeland, What Happened from the Cross to the Throne (Fort Worth, TX: Kenneth Copeland Ministries, 1990), audiotape #02-0017.

· **Benny Hinn**

"And let me add this: **Had the Holy Spirit not been with Jesus, He would have sinned.** That's right, it was the Holy Spirit that was the power that kept Him pure. He was not only sent from heaven, but **He was called the Son of Man—and as such He was capable of sinning…**Without the Holy Ghost, Jesus would have never have made it…**Can you imagine Christ headed for the grave, knowing He would remain there forever, if the Holy Ghost would change**

His mind about raising Him from the dead?" (Benny Hinn, Good Morning, Holy Spirit (Nashville: Thomas Nelson, 1990), 135-36.

· **Copeland**

"Here's where we're gonna depart from ordinary church: Now, you see, God is injecting His Word into the earth to produce this Jesus—these faith-filled words that framed the image that's in Him... **He can't just walk onto the earth and say, "Let it be!" because He doesn't have the right. He had to sneak it in here around the god of this world that was blockin' every way that he possibly could.**" (Kenneth Copeland, The Image of God in You III (Fort Worth, TX: Kenneth Copeland Ministries, 1989), audiotape #01-1403, side 2.

"God was making promises to Jesus, and Jesus wasn't even there. But, you see, God deals with things that are not yet as though they already were. That's the way He gets them to come to pass." (Kenneth Copeland, What Happened from the Cross to the Throne (Fort Worth, TX: Kenneth Copeland Ministries, 1990), audiotape #02-0017.

> ❖ **This is nonsense in light of the fact that we were "chosen in him before the foundation of the world".**

Heresy-----Jesus took on the Nature of Satan

· **Benny Hinn**

"Ladies and gentlemen, the serpent is a symbol of Satan. **Jesus Christ knew the only way He would stop Satan is by becoming one in nature with him.** You say, 'What did you say? What blasphemy is this?' No, you hear this**! He did not take my sin; He became my sin.** Sin is the nature of hell. Sin is what made Satan...It was sin that made Satan. **Jesus said, "I'll be sin! I'll go to the lowest place! I'll go to the origin of it! I won't just take part in it, I'll be the totality of it!**" When Jesus became sin, sir, He took it from A to Z and said, "No more!" Think about this: He became flesh, that flesh might become like Him. He became death, so dying man can live. **He became sin, so sinners can be righteous in Him. He became one with the nature** of Satan, so all those who had the nature of Satan can partake of the nature of God." (Benny Hinn, Benny Hinn program on TBN (December 15, 1990).

· **Kenneth Hagin**

"spiritual death means something more than separation from God. **Spiritual death also means having Satan's nature**...Jesus tasted death—spiritual death—for every man." (Kenneth E. Hagin, The Name of Jesus (Tulsa, OK: Kenneth Hagin Ministries, 1981), 31.

· **Fredrick Price**

"Somewhere between the time He [Jesus] was nailed to the cross and when He was in the Garden of Gethsemane—**somewhere in there—He died spiritually. Personally, I believe it was while He was in the garden.**" (Frederick K. C. Price, Identification #3 (Inglewood, CA: Ever Increasing Faith Ministries, 1980), tape #FP545, side 1.

· **Copeland:**

"The righteousness of God was made to be sin. **He accepted the sin nature of Satan in His own spirit.** And at the moment that He did so, He cried, "My God, My God, why hast thou forsaken Me?" You don't know what happened at the cross. Why do you think Moses, upon instruction of God, raised the serpent upon that pole instead of a lamb? That used to bug me. I said, "Why in the world would you want to put a snake up there—the sign of Satan? Why didn't you put a lamb on that pole?" And the Lord said, "**Because it was a sign of Satan that was hanging on the cross.**" He said, "**I accepted, in My own spirit, spiritual death; and the light was turned off.**" (Kenneth Copeland, What Happened from the Cross to the Throne (Fort Worth, TX: Kenneth Copeland Ministries, 1990), audiotape #02-0017, side 2.

> ❖ **I would remind you that it was not Jesus who took upon himself the nature of sin, for the Bible clearly tells us about the connection between Jesus and SIN;-------**

---------**Isaiah 53**-----"for THE LORD hath laid on him, the iniquities of us all". Just as the High Priest of Israel laid his hands on the

Passover Lamb and symbolically transferred the sins of Israel to the Passover Lamb, so the Father has transferred our sins to his son, and they have been remitted at the Cross". As the Apostle Paul exclaims---"even Christ our Passover is sacrificed for us". There is NOTHING that the Word of Faith heretics will not do or say to demote Christ in his nature. They are FILLED WITH WICKEDNESS. They are violent in doctrine. According to the book of Hebrews 6;4-6----THEY CANNOT BE SAVED!

John Hagee---the very SPECIAL heretic

"This book will expose the sins of the fathers and the vicious abuse of the Jewish people. *In Defense of Israel* will shake Christian theology. It scripturally proves that the Jewish people as a whole did not reject Jesus as Messiah. It will also prove that Jesus did not come to earth to be the Messiah. It will prove that there was a Calvary conspiracy between Rome, the high priest, and Herod to execute Jesus as an insurrectionist too dangerous to live. Since Jesus refused by word and deed to claim to be the Messiah, how can the Jews be blamed for rejecting what was never offered? Read this shocking expose, *In Defense of Israel*"----John Hagee

Dan 9:24-10:1

24 "Seventy 'sevens' are decreed for your people and your holy city to finish transgression, to put an end to sin, to atone for wickedness, to bring in everlasting righteousness, to seal up vision and prophecy and to anoint the most holy.

*25 "Know and understand this: From the issuing of the decree to restore and rebuild Jerusalem **until the Anointed One, the ruler, comes, there will be seven 'sevens,' and sixty-two 'sevens.'** It will be rebuilt with streets and a trench, but in times of trouble.*

*26 After the sixty-two 'sevens,' **the Anointed One will be cut off** and will have nothing. The people of the ruler who will come will destroy the city and the sanctuary. The end will come like a flood: War will continue until the end, and desolations have been decreed.*

27 He will confirm a covenant with many for one 'seven.' In the middle of the 'seven' he will put an end to sacrifice and offering. And on a wing [of the temple] he will set up an abomination that causes desolation, until the end that is decreed is poured out on him."

❖ **This explicit prophecy from the book of Daniel was the very reason that the Jews, in the Days of King Herod, were LOOKING FOR the coming of Messiah. It was the very reason that righteous Simeon was assured that he would live to lay eyes upon Messiah and to prophesy. The notion that the Jews are innocent of their rejection of Messiah is rank heresy.**

<u>Ps 2:2-3</u>

2 The kings of the earth take their stand

and the rulers gather together

against the LORD

and against his Anointed One.

3 "Let us break their chains," they say,

"and throw off their fetters."

❖ **Note the words "and throw off their fetters". This is the very intent of John Hagee----to throw off the fetters of the Word of God.**

<u>John 4:25-26</u>

25 The woman said, "I know that Messiah" (called Christ) "is coming. When he comes, he will explain everything to us."

26 Then Jesus declared, "I who speak to you am he."

❖ **Is there a verse in the entire New Testament that is more clear than this?**

<u>Matt 16:13-20</u>

13 When Jesus came to the region of Caesarea Philippi, he asked his disciples, "Who do people say the Son of Man is?"

14 They replied, "Some say John the Baptist; others say Elijah; and still others, Jeremiah or one of the prophets."

15 "But what about you?" he asked. "Who do you say I am?"

16 Simon Peter answered, "You are the Christ, the Son of the living God."

17 Jesus replied, "Blessed are you, Simon son of Jonah, for this was not revealed to you by man, but by my Father in heaven.

18 And I tell you that you are Peter, and on this rock I will build my church, and the gates of Hades will not overcome it.

19 I will give you the keys of the kingdom of heaven; whatever you bind on earth will be bound in heaven, and whatever you loose on earth will be loosed in heaven."

20 Then he warned his disciples not to tell anyone that he was the Christ. NIV

<u>Acts 2:36</u>

36 "Therefore let all Israel be assured of this: God has made this Jesus, whom you crucified, both Lord and Christ."NIV

<u>John 20:30-31</u>

*30 Jesus did many other miraculous signs in the presence of his disciples, which are not recorded in this book. 31 **But these are written that you may believe that Jesus is the Christ, the Son of God,** and that by believing you may have life in his name. NIV*

<u>John 12:37-41</u>

37 Even after Jesus had done all these miraculous signs in their presence, they still would not believe in him.

38 This was to fulfill the word of Isaiah the prophet:

"Lord, who has believed our message

and to whom has the arm of the Lord been revealed?"

39 For this reason they could not believe, because, as Isaiah says elsewhere:

40 "He has blinded their eyes

and deadened their hearts,

so they can neither see with their eyes,

nor understand with their hearts,

nor turn-and I would heal them."

<u>Rom 9:2-5</u>

3 For I could wish that I myself were cursed and cut off from Christ for the sake of my brothers, those of my own race,

4 the people of Israel. Theirs is the adoption as sons; theirs the divine glory, the covenants, the receiving of the law, the temple worship and the promises.

*5 Theirs are the patriarchs, and from them is traced the human ancestry of Christ, **who is God over all, forever praised! Amen.***

❖ **John Hagee is a heretic, not because I say so, but by any reasonable interpretation of the word "heretic", John Hagee clearly meets the criteria. Jesus said "before Abraham was----I AM". "I AM" is the very name of God. Jesus is GOD and showed himself to be so by his works and by his own declaration. As it is with the followers of other heretics, so it is with those who follow the teachings of John Hagee------they will perish together.**

John Hagee is well admired by the government of Israel for his persistent PANDERING to the Jews. His lust for adoration has taken him beyond the brink. Instead of presenting the Gospel

of Jesus Christ to the Jewish people [which was the desperate desire of the Apostle Paul], he has taken them headlong to the slaughtering floor, and as the scape goat would have it-----has returned to the holding pin to gather more.

Ezek 14:9-10

9 And if the prophet be deceived when he hath spoken a thing, I the LORD have deceived that prophet, and I will stretch out my hand upon him, and will destroy him from the midst of my people Israel.

10 And they shall bear the punishment of their iniquity: **the punishment of the prophet shall be even as the punishment of him that seeketh unto him;** *KJV*

God is very clear about this business of following after a FALSE PROPHET. Those who do so are NEVER INNOCENT. They will suffer the PIT just like their human Idol.

CHAPTER IX

PROSPERITY PIMPS

Along with the many atonement heresies of the Word of Faith Movement, is the false "PROSPERITY DOCTRINE". There are many in the Church today who do not cross the line into heresy in their teaching, but certainly can be appropriately labeled as FALSE TEACHERS. Some go so far as to say that it is a SIN to be poor. One [Fredrick K.C. Price] even asks "do you think that the Holy Spirit wants to live in a body where he cannot see out the windows[eyes]". In other words, the Holy Spirit does not want to dwell in the lives of the physically infirmed, according to Fredrick K.C. Price and many others of the Word of Faith Movement.

Prosperity proponents are not all the same. They range from those who simply appeal for the TITHE, making claims of divine provision based on one's faithfulness to this Old Testament law, to those who use threats and intimidation to coerce giving. The Prosperity Gospel has made its way into Churches around the world, not as a vehicle for spreading the Gospel and provisions for the poor, but as a vehicle to personal prosperity. Spiritual growth is of little concern. In the continent of Africa, where I minister, it is not unusual to find many, many souls who live in fear of the judgment of God for the "crime" of "not paying tithe". There is even a Special evening set aside in Uganda, for the express purpose of purchasing God's Favor in the following year. This special evening is called "Passover", never mind that New Years eve is definitely NOT Passover. I have jokingly stated "the reason they call New Years eve "Passover "is because all the people gather into a big stadium to "pass over" their wallets to those greedy preachers of the Prosperity Gospel. People save money all year long so that they can present the largest offering possible on "Passover eve [New Years]" , thereby purchasing their way out of desperate poverty. Need I say that the money goes into the pockets of organizing local pastors.

"Anointed" prosperity preachers prowl the villages looking for ignorant local pastors to hold meetings to "break the curse of poverty" off of the lives of the very poor. People bring their only clothing, beds, chickens, goats, grain, land deeds------anything they can offer, so that a GREEDY GOD might be appeased and grant his people enough to eat in the near future. If someone SHOULD realize some small amount of money or blessing, the news travels far and wide and lends to perpetuate this christianized spiritual WITCHCRAFT. So why am I talking about Africa? Because these notions were brought to Africa by the likes of Creflo Dollar. Mr. Dollar came to Uganda a couple of years ago. He came to break the SPIRIT OF POVERTY off of Uganda. Since Mr. Dollar's visit, the Uganda Shilling has fallen 25 % in value and continues to decline. The moral of that story?----invite Creflo Dollar to your country and become twenty five percent poorer-----such a deal! Benny Hinn came to Uganda two years ago. The Ugandan organizers of his grand appearance were required to donate fifty dollars for the privilege of helping to organize. I'm still trying to figure this one out-------so, now you PAY your employer for the privilege of working for him?------hmmmmm? John Avanzini has told the story many times about how he collected offerings from desperately poor Africans. He tells of bedding, and furniture being lowered down from the Church balcony and personal belongings piled up to the point that the local pastor had to command "ENOUGH----ENOUGH".

The root of this DOCTRINE OF GREED is America. This is the birthplace of the HEALTH AND WEALTH gospel. It is a direct descendent of the growing pressure to TITHE. It has become a spiritual PONZI SCHEME. Many surveys have been commissioned by the Churches of America to ascertain the very best way to raise money in the Church. The resounding answer is "TITHING". If you can convince enough people to tithe, then you are set to develop projects that would otherwise be unpredictable in terms of success or failure. Another method of gathering money is through the practice of "pledges" over and above the tithe.

So the question is, "how does a pastor convince a person to tithe"? The answer is in the Old Testament, in particular the passage in Malachi chapter three. We have already looked at this passage and found it UNFIT for the Church of Jesus Christ. The very motive of tithe is "if you give----you will get, and if you don't give, well----?????". The doctrine of TITHE is at enmity with the Cross. It is spiritual ADULTRY. It is the ENEMY OF THE CROSS. It is a GIGANTIC FARCE!

Stepping beyond the tithe, there is a doctrine of "SOWING and REAPING". No---it is not the Biblical sowing and reaping that I am speaking of, for the motivation for THIS "sowing and reaping", is PERPETUAL INCREASE, not for the propagation of the Gospel, but for the express WANTS of greedy Christians. Church leaders play on that greed and use it as a tool to convince people to give----sometimes beyond their financial ability, even to the point of using their credit cards if no money is available in their checking account. "Just step out in faith----God wants you to make that pledge even if you don't have the money right now" plead the PIMPS.

The Prosperity Pimps of Christian broadcasting are the very worst. They make promises of manifold blessings for your donations----"God has given me a vision of a certain lady who is watching this program right now----I can literally SEE your face. You're asking yourself right now----is he talking to me? If you asked that question then the answer is YES----YES.. It's you m'am, It's you. Step over to your desk and pull out that check book and write a sacrificial check for one thousand dollars to WANTYOBUCK MINISTRIES----quickly now----quickly, while the Hundred Fold Spirit is moving". Can't ya just see it?---Can't ya just hear it? Thousands of well meaning Christians have lost

EVERYTHING in these ministries because their hearts were not right in the understanding of "giving".

A SCRIPTURAL REBUTTAL OF THE PROSPERITY GOSPEL

1 Timothy 6:1-11

1 Let as many servants as are under the yoke count their own masters worthy of all honour, that the name of God and his doctrine be not blasphemed.

2 And they that have believing masters, let them not despise them, because they are brethren; but rather do them service, because they are faithful and beloved, partakers of the benefit. These things teach and exhort.

3 If any man teach otherwise, and consent not to wholesome words, even the words of our Lord Jesus Christ, and to the doctrine which is according to godliness;

4 He is proud, knowing nothing, but doting about questions and strifes of words, whereof cometh envy, strife, railings, evil surmisings,

*5 Perverse disputings of men of corrupt minds, and destitute of the truth, **supposing that gain is godliness: from such withdraw thyself.***

6 But godliness with contentment is great gain.

7 For we brought nothing into this world, and it is certain we can carry nothing out.

*8 And **having food and raiment let us be therewith content.***

*9 But **they that will be rich fall into temptation and a snare**, and into many foolish and hurtful lusts, which drown men in destruction and perdition.*

10 For the love of money is the root of all evil: which while some coveted after, they have erred from the faith, and pierced themselves through with many sorrows.

11 But thou, O man of God, **flee these things; and follow after righteousness, godliness, faith, love, patience, meekness.**

Luke 4:18

18 The Spirit of the Lord is upon me, **because he hath anointed me to preach the gospel to the poor;** *he hath sent me to heal the brokenhearted, to preach deliverance to the captives, and recovering of sight to the blind, to set at liberty them that are bruised,*

Luke 6:20

20 And he lifted up his eyes on his disciples, and said, **Blessed be ye poor:** *for yours is the kingdom of God.*

Luke 12:15

15 And he said unto them, **Take heed, and beware of covetousness: for a man's life consisteth not in the abundance of the things which he possesseth.**

Matt.6:22-27

22 And he said unto his disciples, Therefore I say unto you, **Take no thought for your life, what ye shall eat; neither for the body, what ye shall put on.**

23 The life is more than meat, and the body is more than raiment.

24 Consider the ravens: for they neither sow nor reap; which neither have storehouse nor barn; and God feedeth them: how much more are ye better than the fowls?

25 And which of you with taking thought can add to his stature one cubit?

26 If ye then be not able to do that thing which is least, why take ye thought for the rest?

27 Consider the lilies how they grow: they toil not, they spin not; and yet I say unto you, that Solamon in all his glory was not arrayed like one of these.

28 If then God so clothe the grass, which is to day in the field, and tomorrow is cast into the oven; **how much more will he clothe you, O ye of little faith?**

29 And seek not ye what ye shall eat, or what ye shall drink, neither be ye of doubtful mind.

30 For all these things do the nations of the world seek after: and your Father knoweth that ye have need of these things.

31 But rather seek ye the kingdom of God; and all these things shall be added unto you.

<u>Luke 12:33-34</u>

33 Sell that ye have, and give alms; provide yourselves bags which wax not old, a treasure in the heavens that faileth not, where no thief approacheth, neither moth corrupteth.

34 *For where your treasure is, there will your heart be also.*

Luke 16:13

13 No servant can serve two masters: for either he will hate the one, and love the other; or else he will hold to the one, and despise the other. **Ye cannot serve God and mammon.**

<u>Luke 16:15</u>

15 And he said unto them, Ye are they which justify yourselves before men; but God knoweth your hearts: **for that which is highly esteemed among men is abomination in the sight of God.**

Matthew 6:19-20

19 Lay not up for yourselves treasures upon earth, where moth and rust doth corrupt, and where thieves break through and steal:

20 But lay up for yourselves treasures in heaven, where neither moth nor rust doth corrupt, and where thieves do not break through nor steal:

Mark 10:21

21 Then Jesus beholding him loved him, and said unto him, One thing thou lackest: **go thy way, sell whatsoever thou hast, and give to the poor, and thou shalt have treasure in heaven: and come, take up the cross, and follow me.**

Mark 10:25

25 It is easier for a camel to go through the eye of a needle, than for a rich man to enter into the kingdom of God

Hebrews 13:5

5 Let your conversation be without covetousness; **and be content with such things as ye have:** *for he hath said, I will never leave thee, nor forsake thee.*

Philippians 4:11-13

11 Not that I speak in respect of want: for I have learned, in **whatsoever state I am, therewith to be content.**

12 I know both how to be abased, and I know how to abound: everywhere and in all things I am instructed both to be full and to be hungry, both to abound and to suffer need.

13 I can do all things through Christ which strengthened me.

Philippians 4:19

19 But my God shall supply all your need *according to his riches in glory by Christ Jesus.*

Proverbs 23:4-5

4 **Labour not to be rich:** *cease from thine own wisdom.*

5 **Wilt thou set thine eyes upon that which is not?** *for riches certainly make themselves wings; they fly away as an eagle toward heaven.*

Proverbs 30:7-9

7Two things have I required of thee; deny me them not before I die:

8 *Remove far from me vanity and lies:* **give me neither poverty nor riches; feed me with food convenient for me:**

9 **Lest I be full, and deny thee, and say, Who is the LORD? or lest I be poor, and steal, and take the name of my God in vain.**

Matthew 16:24-26

24Then said Jesus unto his disciples, If any man will come after me, **let him deny himself, and take up his cross, and follow me.**

25 For whosoever will save his life shall lose it: and whosoever will lose his life for my sake shall find it.

26 **For what is a man profited, if he shall gain the whole world, and lose his own soul?** *or what shall a man give in exchange for his soul?*

Luke 14:33

18 So likewise, **whosoever he be of you that forsaketh not all that he hath, he cannot be my disciple.**

Luke 6:38

38 Give, and it shall be given unto you; good measure, pressed down, and shaken together, and running over, shall men give into your bosom. **For with the same measure that ye mete withal it shall be measured to you again.**

1 Corinthians 4:9-13

9For I think that God hath set forth us the apostles last, as it were appointed to death: for we are made a spectacle unto the world, and to angels, and to men.

10 We are fools for Christ's sake, but ye are wise in Christ; we are weak, but ye are strong; ye are honorable, but we are despised.

11 Even unto this present hour we both hunger, and thirst, and are naked, and are buffeted, and have no certain dwelling place;

12 And labour, working with our own hands: being reviled, we bless; being persecuted, we suffer it:

13 Being defamed, we entreat: we are made as the filth of the world, and are the off scouring of all things unto this day.

Matthew 8:20

20 And Jesus saith unto him, The foxes have holes, and the birds of the air have nests; **but the Son of man hath not where to lay his head.**

Mark 10:17-31

17 And when he was gone forth into the way, there came one running, and kneeled to him, and asked him, Good Master, what shall I do that I may inherit eternal life?

18 And Jesus said unto him, Why callest thou me good? there is none good but one, that is, God.

19 Thou knowest the commandments, Do not commit adultery, Do not kill, Do not steal, Do not bear false witness, Defraud not, Honour thy father and mother.

20 And he answered and said unto him, Master, all these have I observed from my youth.

21 Then Jesus beholding him loved him, and said unto him, One thing thou lackest: go thy way, **sell whatsoever thou hast, and give to the** poor, and thou shalt have treasure in heaven: and come, take up the cross, and follow me.

22 And he was sad at that saying, and went away grieved: for he had great possessions.

23 And Jesus looked round about, and saith unto his disciples, How hardly shall they that have riches enter into the kingdom of God!

24 And the disciples were astonished at his words. But Jesus answereth again, and saith unto them, Children, how hard is it for them that trust in riches to enter into the kingdom of God!

25 It is easier for a camel to go through the eye of a needle, than for a rich man to enter into the kingdom of God.

26 And they were astonished out of measure, saying among themselves, Who then can be saved?

27 And Jesus looking upon them saith, With men it is impossible, but not with God: for with God all things are possible.

28 Then Peter began to say unto him, Lo, we have left all, and have followed thee.

29 And Jesus answered and said, Verily I say unto you, There is no man that hath left house, or brethren, or sisters, or father, or mother, or wife, or children, or lands, for my sake, and the gospel's,

30 But he shall receive an hundredfold now in this time, houses, and brethren, and sisters, and mothers, and children, and lands, with persecutions; and in the world to come eternal life.

31 But many that are first shall be last; and the last first.

2 Corinthians 9:1

1 For as touching the ministering to the saints, it is superfluous for me to write to you:

2 Corinthians 9:5-6

5 Therefore I thought it necessary to exhort the brethren, that they would go before unto you, and make up before hand your bounty, whereof ye had notice before, that the same might be ready, as a matter of bounty, and not as of covetousness.

6 But this I say, He which soweth sparingly shall reap also sparingly; **and he which soweth bountifully shall reap also bountifully.**

Mark 4:3-9

3 Hearken; Behold, there went out a sower to sow:

4 And it came to pass, as he sowed, some fell by the way side, and the fowls of the air came and devoured it up.

5 And some fell on stony ground, where it had not much earth; and immediately it sprang up, because it had no depth of earth:

6 But when the sun was up, it was scorched; and because it had no root, it withered away.

7 **And some fell among thorns, and the thorns grew up, and choked it, and it yielded no fruit.**

8 And other fell on good ground, and did yield fruit that sprang up and increased; and brought forth, some thirty, and some sixty, and some an hundred.

9 And he said unto them, He that hath ears to hear, let him hear.

10 And when he was alone, they that were about him with the twelve asked of him the parable.

11 And he said unto them, Unto you it is given to know the mystery of the kingdom of God: but unto them that are without, all these things are done in parables:

12 That seeing they may see, and not perceive; and hearing they may hear, and not understand; lest at any time they should be converted, and their sins should be forgiven them.

13 And he said unto them, Know ye not this parable? and how then will ye know all parables?

14 The sower soweth the word.

15 And these are they by the way side, where the word is sown; but when they have heard, Satan cometh immediately, and taketh away the word that was sown in their hearts.

16 And these are they likewise which are sown on stony ground; who, when they have heard the word, immediately receive it with gladness;

17 And have no root in themselves, and so endure but for a time: afterward, when affliction or persecution ariseth for the word's sake, immediately they are offended.

*18 **And these are they which are sown among thorns; such as hear the word,***

*19 **And the cares of this world, and the deceitfulness of riches, and the lusts of other things entering in, choke the word, and it becometh unfruitful.***

20 And these are they which are sown on good ground; such as hear the word, and receive it, and bring forth fruit, some thirtyfold, some sixty, and some an hundred. KJV

<u>Habakkuk 3:17-18</u>

17 Although the fig tree shall not blossom, neither shall fruit be in the vines; the labour of the olive shall fail, and the fields shall yield no meat; the flock shall be cut off from the fold, and there shall be no herd in the stalls:

*18 **Yet I will rejoice in the LORD, I will joy in the God of my salvation.***

I could easily show an exhaustive list of those well known **PROSPERITY PIMPS** that are **RAPING** the Church and re-directing needed funds that could have gone to hungry Christians around the world. There are simply too many to count. As I write this

215

book, I am pleading with friends to help me raise money for a desperate village woman in Uganda. I will paste the e-letter that I received just today from a brother in Entebbe. He has set aside building his own home for his family so that he can build a modest house for this poor woman, so that she and her children can have a place to sleep, free from the elements-----

Dedicated to Okurut Robert:

Ps 41:1-3

41:1 Blessed is he that considereth the poor: the LORD will deliver him in time of trouble.

2 The LORD will preserve him, and keep him alive; and he shall be blessed upon the earth: and thou wilt not deliver him unto the will of his enemies.

3 The LORD will strengthen him upon the bed of languishing: thou wilt make all his bed in his sickness. **KJV**

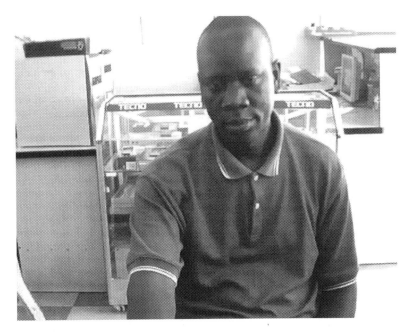

On Thu, Dec 30, 2010 at 9:01 AM, okurut Robert [address deleted] wrote:

Danny haven't got the wall hangings and Andrews is off hope to see him in the new year. However receive the photos of the widow, her house, the inside of the house, my young brother laying bricks, and her little grand children plas her daughter with twins all living together in the compound and she sleeps with about 5 children in that hut all below 10 years. she also has two grown up sons but they are mentally retarded. and they grew up in an abnormal way they are very tall and weak they both have interlocking bent legs inside the hut where you see her seated is her bed it is just a polythene paper with some grass pressed inside fany enough she is atal woman and the polythene bag which serves as mattress is just half way to her wast. Thank you so much. Robert

Here's mamma at the site of her New HOUSE being built thanks to the gifts of Okurut Robert and friends of the New Testament Fellowship of Winston Salem North Carolina. Okurut Robert discovered this woman in a village near his home about fifteen miles from Mbale. He was so disturbed by what he saw that he halted construction of his own family home and vowed to build this poor woman a house BEFORE he does any further work on his own home. Note the dilapidated hut in the background. Imagine what it would be like to move from that mud hut into a brick house.

Pastor Bita James Oloo

His friends call him "Jimmy". He is a young pastor who ministers from Entebbe to Tororo in Eastern Uganda. Jimmy teaches New Testament Christianity in the cities and villages of Uganda. Jimmy has a BRICK MAKING business in his village in East Uganda. He makes bricks and sells them. He and his wife Regina make them by hand. He uses the proceeds to fund his ministry. His passion is for teaching the truth of the New Testament to those who have not heard. Many local people have been ravaged by the "Prosperity Pimps" who stalk the villages in pursuit of loot. They tell people that they can be healed of AIDS if only they will give everything they have to "god"----eh eh----themselves. The people are often terrorized by the prospect of increasing poverty if they do not PAY THE TITHE. These poor people bring their livestock, even the little furniture and goods they may have, and give it to the "prosperity pimps" in hope of healing, or a better life, and wealth. Needless to say----they are ALL disappointed in the results. Pastor Oloo is in a desperate battle to push back at this travesty. He is OBSESSED with the TRUTH. He is pleading for Bibles to give to the young men who he is training to go into the villages with the GOOD NEWS.

Figure 1 Mrs. Regina Bita

Figure 2 At home in the village---Pastor Jimmy and Regina. Regina is pregnant with their first child

Figure 3 Covering the bricks with elephant grass to protect them from the rain

These things are suppose to CRUSH US. They are suppose to cause us to grieve, but we know nothing of the tragic conditions of those for whom Christ died. WHY----because we have been taken down a four lane highway to the pursuit of STUFF, and have failed to turn on to that goat path that leads to an impoverished village in Eastern Uganda.

Rev 3:14-4:1

14 "To the angel of the church in Laodicea write:

These are the words of the Amen, the faithful and true witness, the ruler of God's creation.

15 I know your deeds, **that you are neither cold nor hot.** I wish you were either one or the other!

16 So, because you are lukewarm-neither hot nor cold-I am about to spit you out of my mouth.

17 You say, '**I am rich; I have acquired wealth and do not need a thing.**' But you do not realize that **you are wretched, pitiful, poor, blind and naked.**

18 I counsel you to buy from me gold refined in the fire, so you can become rich; and white clothes to wear, so you can cover your shameful nakedness; and salve to put on your eyes, so you can see. 19 Those whom I love I rebuke and discipline. So be earnest, and repent.

20 Here I am! I stand at the door and knock. If anyone hears my voice and opens the door, I will come in and eat with him, and he with me.

21 To him who overcomes, I will give the right to sit with me on my throne, just as I overcame and sat down with my Father on his throne.

22 He who has an ear, let him hear what the Spirit says to the churches." NIV

Of the seven Churches of Asia, Laodicea stands alone. She is absolutely unique. She bears no suffering or persecution. There is no hunger or tribulation. Yet she is the most disgusting Church of the Ages. She is the ONLY Church of the ages to which the Lord has absolutely NOTHING good to say. What a repulsive thought! She is the product of her mother Babylon, who proudly stands among the nations and declares "I am a queen and have need of nothing" [Rev.18]. She boasts her wealth as a sign of God's approval. She stoops to giving her miserly contributions to her sibling Churches in poor nations and slaps herself on the back for her bland effort. While her brothers and sisters dig for roots to eat in equatorial Africa, she ENTERTAINS her lofty attendees. She is GRAND indeed. She is the expression of Babylon the Great----the Mother of Harlots. She is the Church of America.

Yet, in God's eyes, she is the poorest of all. She is destitute in values. She is corrupted by her own wealth and beauty. Her days are spent looking in the mirror and seeing only her own loveliness. She is narcissistic, blind and deaf at the same time. Her institutions are incestuous. She smells of dainty odours, but is wrapped in rotting flesh. At the same time, she is INSANE. Her doctrines are corrupted with deceit. Her master is that same Crowning Cherub who served as Heaven's Minister of Music. Only the strong medication of DESTRUCTION and POVERTY can return her to a right mind.

CHAPTER X

WHAT DOES YOUR APOSTLE LOOK LIKE?

If your APOSTLE speaks contrary to these words----She/he IS NO APOSTLE OF CHRIST-----and MUST BE REJECTED!!!

<u>1 Tim 6:3-12</u>

3 If any man teach otherwise, and consent not to wholesome words, even the words of our Lord Jesus Christ, and to the doctrine which is according to godliness;

4 He is proud, knowing nothing, but doting about questions and strifes of words, whereof cometh envy, strife, railings, evil surmisings,

5 Perverse disputings of men of corrupt minds, ***and destitute of the truth, supposing that gain is godliness: from such withdraw thyself.***

6 But godliness with contentment is great gain.

7 For we brought nothing into this world, and it is certain we can carry nothing out.

8 And having food and raiment let us be therewith content.

9 But they that will be rich fall into temptation and a snare, and into many foolish and hurtful lusts, which drown men in destruction and perdition.

10 For the love of money is the root of all evil: which while some coveted after, they have erred from the faith, and pierced themselves through with many sorrows.

11 But thou, O man of God, flee these things; and follow after righteousness, godliness, faith, love, patience, meekness

12 Fight the good fight of faith, lay hold on eternal life, whereunto thou art also called, and hast professed a good profession before many witnesses. KJV

Phil 4:10-13

10 But I rejoiced in the Lord greatly, that now at the last your care of me hath flourished again; wherein ye were also careful, but ye lacked opportunity.

11 Not that I speak in respect of want: for I have learned, in whatsoever state I am, therewith to be content.

12 I know both how to be abased, and I know how to abound: everywhere and in all things I am instructed both to be full and to be hungry, both to abound and to suffer need. KJV

2 Cor 11:24-12:1

24 Of the Jews five times received I forty stripes save one.

25 Thrice was I beaten with rods, once was I stoned, thrice I suffered shipwreck, a night and a day I have been in the deep;

26 In journeyings often, in perils of waters, in perils of robbers, in perils by mine own countrymen, in perils by the heathen, in perils in the city, in perils in the wilderness, in perils in the sea, in perils among false brethren;

27 In weariness and painfulness, in watchings often, in hunger and thirst, in fastings often, in cold and nakedness.

28 Beside those things that are without, that which cometh upon me daily, the care of all the churches.

29 Who is weak, and I am not weak? who is offended, and I burn not?

30 If I must needs glory, I will glory of the things which concern mine infirmities.

31 The God and Father of our Lord Jesus Christ, which is blessed for evermore, knoweth that I lie not.

32 In Damascus the governor under Aretas the king kept the city of the Damascenes with a garrison, desirous to apprehend me:

33 And through a window in a basket was I let down by the wall, and escaped his hands. KJV

❖ **THIS IS THE ATTITUDE OF A TRUE APOSTLE-------- anything else is FALSE!**

Is your "APOSTLE"------------------------**a MAN?**

Is your "Apostle"--------------------------**a JEW?**

Was your "Apostle"---------------------**personally chosen by Jesus Christ?**

Is your "Apostle"------------------------**numbered among TWELVE?**

Is the doctrine of your "Apostle"-------**infallible?**

Is your "Apostle's name"---------------**written on the foundations of Heaven?**

If NOT------------------------------------**he/she is no Apostle at all!!**

Rev 21:12-14

12 And had a wall great and high, and had twelve gates, and at the gates twelve angels, and names written thereon, which are the names of the twelve tribes of the children of Israel:

13 On the east three gates; on the north three gates; on the south three gates; and on the west three gates.

14 And the wall of the city had twelve foundations, and in them the names of the twelve apostles of the Lamb

There must be tens of thousands of so called "apostles" in the earth today. The Reformers of the Church age absolutely shunned such a title because of their strong belief that only the Apostles of the New Testament fully met the Biblical requirements of Apostleship, whereas, those who would follow could not. In Uganda, where I teach New Testament Christianity and Bible Prophecy, there are so many "apostles" that they are stumbling all over one another. Each one teaching and promoting a doctrine estranged from the other. It is simply impossible that these men are legitimate in their claims to "apostleship". They argue about matters ranging from TRIVIAL NONSENSE to issues central to the Christian Faith. Each one demanding his/her way. Some to the exclusion of all others. They greet each other warmly on the street, and turn to whisper their disapproval of the other as soon as they reach a comfortable distance. There is only ONE SURE TEST of the authenticity of an Apostle-----"are his teachings infallible"? Can even one small error be found in his doctrine? If so----he/she is NOT AN APOSTLE of Jesus Christ!

CHAPTER XI

The Role of Women in the Church

It is clearly authorized in the New Testament, that women should teach other women and children in the church. In today's Church, that amounts to upward of seventy percent of the population of the Church in Universal terms. That has never been an issue in the Church then or now. The issue is this----"shall a woman teach MEN in the assembly of the Church"? There is disagreement and sometimes downright hostility surrounding this question. Let's take a look at what the New Testament has to say about this matter. Then we will look at some contributing factors and information that will "hopefully" expose the source of that polarization between the doctrinal factions.

Gen 2:7-3:1

7 the LORD God formed the man from the dust of the ground and breathed into his nostrils the breath of life, and the man became a living being.

8 Now the LORD God had planted a garden in the east, in Eden; and there he put the man he had formed.

*9 And the LORD God made all kinds of trees grow out of the ground--trees that were pleasing to the eye and good for food. In the middle of the garden were the tree of life **and the tree of the knowledge of good and evil.***

10 A river watering the garden flowed from Eden; from there it was separated into four headwaters.

11 The name of the first is the Pishon; it winds through the entire land of Havilah, where there is gold.

12(The gold of that land is good; aromatic resin and onyx are also there.)

13 The name of the second river is the Gihon; it winds through the entire land of Cush.

14 The name of the third river is the Tigris; it runs along the east side of Asshur. And the fourth river is the Euphrates.

15 The LORD God took the man and put him in the Garden of Eden to work it and take care of it.

16 And the LORD God commanded the man, **"You are free to eat from any tree in the garden;**

17 but you must not eat from the tree of the knowledge of good and evil, for when you eat of it you will surely die."

> ❖ **Please note that it was unto ADAM that this first command was given, and that the Woman had not yet been created. It was Adam's principle responsibility to obey the command of God.**

18 The LORD God said, "It is not good for the man to be alone. **I will make a helper suitable for him."**

> ❖ **In this verse, the Lord has determined to create "a helper" for Adam. He has not determined to make a "slave" but a HELPER.**

19 Now the LORD God had formed out of the ground all the beasts of the field and all the birds of the air. He brought them to the man to see what he would name them; and whatever the man called each living creature, that was its name.

20 So the man gave names to all the livestock, the birds of the air and all the beasts of the field.

But for Adam no suitable helper was found.

21 So the LORD God caused the man to fall into a deep sleep; and while he was sleeping, he took one of the man's ribs and closed up the place with flesh.

*22 **Then the LORD God made a woman from the rib he had taken out of the man, and he brought her to the man.***

23 The man said,

"This is now bone of my bones

and flesh of my flesh;

she shall be called 'woman,'

for she was taken out of man."

❖ **Note that it is ADAM that has named woman and not God himself. It is Adam whom God has given to establish her identity.**

24 For this reason a man will leave his father and mother and be united to his wife, and they will become one flesh.

25 The man and his wife were both naked, and they felt no shame.
NIV

<u>1 Tim 2:11-15</u>

11 A woman should learn in quietness and full submission.

12 I do not permit a woman to teach or to have authority over a man; she must be silent.

*13 **For Adam was formed first, then Eve.***

14 And Adam was not the one deceived; it was the woman who was deceived and became a sinner.

15 But women will be saved through childbearing-if they continue in faith, love and holiness with propriety.

> ❖ Note that it is not Adam who was beguiled by the Serpent, rather, he was tempted by EVE. Because Adam was chosen in God to be the head of the woman, he was charged with the full responsibility for their joint venture into rebellion.

<u>1 Tim 2:11-3:1</u>

11 A woman should learn in quietness and full submission.

12 I do not permit a woman to teach or to have authority over a man; she must be silent.

13 For Adam was formed first, then Eve.

14 And Adam was not the one deceived; it was the woman who was deceived and became a sinner.

15 But women will be saved through childbearing-if they continue in faith, love and holiness with propriety.

> ❖ It was not Adam who was deceived, it was the woman. It was the WOMAN who had been beguiled by the serpent. The man was NEVER BEGUILED. He stepped WILLINGLY in to sin.

1 Cor 11:3-10

*3 Now I want you to realize that the head of every man is Christ, **and the head of the woman is man**, and the head of Christ is God.*

4 Every man who prays or prophesies with his head covered dishonors his head.

5 And every woman who prays or prophesies with her head uncovered dishonors her head-it is just as though her head were shaved.

6 If a woman does not cover her head, she should have her hair cut off; and if it is a disgrace for a woman to have her hair cut or shaved off, she should cover her head.

7 A man ought not to cover his head, since he is the image and glory of God; but the woman is the glory of man.

8 For man did not come from woman, but woman from man;

9 neither was man created for woman, but woman for man.

10 For this reason, and because of the angels, the woman ought to have a sign of authority on her head.

> ❖ **These verses clearly show the order of authority in the Church. They are thus;**
>
> **1---the Father**
>
> **2.---the Son**
>
> **3.---Man**
>
> **4.---Woman**

To deny this is tantamount to spiritual rebellion.

<u>Gen 3:1-13</u>

*3:1 Now the serpent was more crafty than any of the wild animals the LORD God had made. He said to the woman, "**Did God really say**, 'You must not eat from any tree in the garden'?"*

2 The woman said to the serpent, "We may eat fruit from the trees in the garden, 3 but God did say, 'You must not eat fruit from the tree that is in the middle of the garden, and you must not touch it, or you will die.'"

4 "You will not surely die," the serpent said to the woman.

5 "For God knows that when you eat of it your eyes will be opened, and you will be like God, knowing good and evil."

*6 When the woman saw that the fruit of the tree **was good for food and pleasing to the eye, and also desirable for gaining wisdom,** she took some and ate it. She also gave some to her husband, who was with her, and he ate it.*

7 Then the eyes of both of them were opened, and they realized they were naked; so they sewed fig leaves together and made coverings for themselves.

❖ **Note there are three reasons for Eve's temptation.**

  1. good for food

  2. pleasing to the eye

  3. desirable for GAINING WISDOM

❖ **It was "wisdom" that "tipped the scale". It was the desire for "knowledge that exceeded her own human capability". In this Biblical fact lies the revelation into WHY it is not given for a woman to teach men in the Church.**

8 Then the man and his wife heard the sound of the LORD God as he was walking in the garden in the cool of the day, and they hid from the LORD God among the trees of the garden.

*9 **But the LORD God called to the man,** "Where are you?"*

❖ **Note that both man and woman heard the voice of God---- yet the Lord spoke specifically to the man. It was THE MAN who was ultimately responsible for what had taken place. Harry Truman said it best---"the BUCK STOPS HERE".**

*10 **He answered,** "I heard you in the garden, and I was afraid because I was naked; so I hid."*

❖ It was "he" that answered and not "She or they". Adam was the one held responsible for the situation, and HE KNEW IT.

11 And he said, "Who told you that you were naked? Have you eaten from the tree that I commanded you not to eat from?"

12 The man said, "The woman you put here with me--she gave me some fruit from the tree, and I ate it."

*13 **Then the LORD God said to the woman,** "What is this you have done?"*

❖ "THEN" the Lord said to the woman-----

The woman said, "The serpent deceived me, and I ate."

❖ Notice how everyone is passing the buck----Adam blames the woman, Eve blames the serpent, but after all is said and done, it is ADAM that bares the responsibility.

1 Peter 3:1-6

*3:1 Wives, **in the same way be submissive to your husbands so that,** if any of them do not believe the word, **they may be won over without words by the behavior of their wives,** 2 when they see the purity and reverence of your lives. 3 Your beauty should not come from outward adornment, such as braided hair and the wearing of gold jewelry and fine clothes.*

4 Instead, it should be that of your inner self, the unfading beauty of a gentle and quiet spirit, which is of great worth in God's sight.

*5 For this is the way the holy women of the past who put their hope in God used to make themselves beautiful. **They were submissive to their own husbands,***

*6 **like Sarah, who obeyed Abraham and called him her master.** You are her daughters if you do what is right and do not give way to fear.*

❖ **Look at the ultimate goal of this passage. It is selfless in motive.** **It is the conversion of the unsaved husband that the Lord is concerned with, and Peter expresses this beautifully in this command.** it surely shows how things come together for ultimate GOOD when God's order is in play.

Eph 5:21-6:1

21 **Submit to one another out of reverence for Christ.**

22 Wives, submit to your husbands as to the Lord.

23 **For the husband is the head of the wife as Christ is the head of the church,** *his body, of which he is the Savior.*

24 Now as the church submits to Christ, so also wives should submit to their husbands in everything.

❖ **This NOT MERELY a "carnal" matter. It is SPIRITUAL! It is a matter of faith----faith and trust in God to know what is best and because of that trust, to obey, not in fear, but in the belief that God knows what he is doing.**

25 Husbands, love your wives, just as Christ loved the church and gave himself up for her

26 to make her holy, cleansing her by the washing with water through the word,

27 and to present her to himself as a radiant church, without stain or wrinkle or any other blemish, but holy and blameless.

28 In this same way, husbands ought to love their wives as their own bodies. He who loves his wife loves himself.

29 After all, no one ever hated his own body, **but he feeds and cares for it, just as Christ does the church-**

30 for we are members of his body.

31 *"For this reason a man will leave his father and mother and be united to his wife, and the two will become one flesh."*

32 *This is a profound mystery-but I am talking about Christ and the church.*

33 **However, each one of you also must love his wife as he loves himself, and the wife must respect her husband.**

<u>Col 3:18-19</u>

18 **Wives, submit to your husbands, as is fitting in the Lord.**

❖ **Again----this is a "spiritual" matter**

19 *Husbands, love your wives and do not be harsh with them. NIV*

<u>Titus 2:3-5</u>

3 *Likewise, teach the older women to be reverent in the way they live, not to be slanderers or addicted to much wine, but to teach what is good.*

4 **Then they can train the younger women to love their husbands and children,**

5 **to be self-controlled and pure, to be busy at home, to be kind, and to be subject to their husbands, so that no one will malign the word of God.**

❖ **And again, this is a spiritual matter.**

<u>1 Tim 3:3-5</u>

4 *He must manage his own family well and see that his children obey him with proper respect.* 5**(If anyone does not know how to manage his own family, how can he take care of God's church? NIV**

1 Tim 3:12-13

12 A deacon must be **the husband of but one wife** and must manage his children and his household well.

13 Those who have served well gain an excellent standing and great assurance in their faith in Christ Jesus.

❖ **This verse is clearly addressed to MEN.**

Gal 3:23-29

23 Before this faith came, we were held prisoners by the law, locked up until faith should be revealed.

24 So the law was put in charge to lead us to Christ that we might be justified by faith.

25 Now that faith has come, we are no longer under the supervision of the law.

26 You are all sons of God through faith in Christ Jesus,

27 for all of you who were baptized into Christ have clothed yourselves with Christ.

28 There is neither Jew nor Greek, slave nor free, male nor female, for you are all one in Christ Jesus.

29 If you belong to Christ, then you are Abraham's seed, and heirs according to the promise.

❖ **This verse is often taken completely out of context with no regard to surrounding scriptural support. This verse speaks specifically to the believers relationship to Christ as their redeemer, and not to the "order of authority" in the Church.**

1 Tim 2:11-3:1

11 A woman should learn in quietness and full submission.

12 I do not permit a woman to teach or to have authority over a man; she must be silent.

13 For Adam was formed first, then Eve.

14 And Adam was not the one deceived; it was the woman who was deceived and became a sinner.

15 But women will be saved through childbearing-if they continue in faith, love and holiness with propriety.

❖ Understanding this portion of scripture is important to both men, and women. The emphasis is on the fact that ADAM WAS FORMED FIRST. He was placed in authority because he was the first created in the image of God.

<u>1 Cor 14:33-15:1</u>

33 For God is not a God of disorder but of peace.

As in all the congregations of the saints,

34 women should remain silent in the churches. They are not allowed to speak, but must be in submission, as the Law says.

35 If they want to inquire about something, they should ask their own husbands at home; for it is disgraceful for a woman to speak in the church.

36 Did the word of God originate with you? Or are you the only people it has reached?

37 If anybody thinks he is a prophet or spiritually gifted, let him acknowledge that what I am writing to you is the Lord's command.

38 If he ignores this, he himself will be ignored.

❖ In order to pronounce one's self as a prophet/prophetess, one must succumb to the admonishment of this passage. The implication is that if one does not submit to these

> **words of Paul, it is a clear indication that he/she is not a true prophet in the Church. To deny this is to deny your own authority.**

39 Therefore, my brothers, be eager to prophesy, and do not forbid speaking in tongues.

*40 **But everything should be done in a fitting and orderly way.***

- ❖ **"ORDER" is the emphasis in this verse.**

<u>1 Cor 11:2-16</u>

*2 I praise you for remembering me in everything **and for holding to the teachings, just as I passed them on to you.***

*3 Now I want you to realize that **the head of every man is Christ, and the head of the woman is man, and the head of Christ is God.***

4 Every man who prays or prophesies with his head covered dishonors his head.

5 And every woman who prays or prophesies with her head uncovered dishonors her head-it is just as though her head were shaved.

6 If a woman does not cover her head, she should have her hair cut off; and if it is a disgrace for a woman to have her hair cut or shaved off, she should cover her head.

7 A man ought not to cover his head, since he is the image and glory of God; but the woman is the glory of man.

8 For man did not come from woman, but woman from man;

9 neither was man created for woman, but woman for man.

10 For this reason, and because of the angels, the woman ought to have a sign of authority on her head.

- ❖ **In this portion, a contrast is made between physical and spiritual adornment. The woman's "covering" is a representation of her understanding of her responsibility to recognize her husband as her authority in the home,**

and likewise----men as the authority in the church. It is simply "GOD'S WAY".

11 In the Lord, however, woman is not independent of man, nor is man independent of woman.

12 For as woman came from man, so also man is born of woman. **But everything comes from God.**

13 Judge for yourselves: Is it proper for a woman to pray to God with her head uncovered?

14 Does not the very nature of things teach you that if a man has long hair, it is a disgrace to him,

15 but that if a woman has long hair, it is her glory? For long hair is given to her as a covering.

16 If anyone wants to be contentious about this, **we have no other practice-nor do the churches of God.**

- ❖ **Some have suggested that the "gender order" in the Church was due to regional customs. It is clear in this statement that no such "custom" influenced the Church. It was and is, the doctrinal mandate, that women are not to teach men nor to exert authority over them "in all the Churches".**

<u>1 Tim 3:8-16</u>

8 Deacons, likewise, **are to be men worthy of respect**, *sincere, not indulging in much wine, and not pursuing dishonest gain.*

9 They must keep hold of the deep truths of the faith with a clear conscience.

10 They must first be tested; and then if there is nothing against them, let them serve as deacons.

11 In the same way, **their wives are to be women worthy of respect**, *not malicious talkers but temperate and trustworthy in everything.*

*12 A deacon must be **the husband of but one wife** and must manage his children and his household well. 13 Those who have served well gain an excellent standing and great assurance in their faith in Christ Jesus.*

14 Although I hope to come to you soon, I am writing you these instructions so that,

15 if I am delayed, you will know how people ought to conduct themselves in God's household, which is the church of the living God, the pillar and foundation of the truth.

16 Beyond all question, the mystery of godliness is great:

<u>*Acts 18:24-26*</u>

24 Meanwhile a Jew named Apollos, a native of Alexandria, came to Ephesus. He was a learned man, with a thorough knowledge of the Scriptures.

25 He had been instructed in the way of the Lord, and he spoke with great fervor and taught about Jesus accurately, though he knew only the baptism of John.

*26 He began to speak boldly in the synagogue. **When Priscilla and Aquila heard him, they invited him to their home and explained to him the way of God more adequately.***

> ❖ **This portion is often used to rebut the notion that women ought not to teach men in the Church. Note that these women invited Apollos into their home in order to teach him a more perfect understanding. The very fact that discretion was used in this manner simply SUPPORTS the fact that women are not to teach men "in the Church". In fact, these women were fully in order by handling the situation in this manner. They acted in the way of Church Mothers and not in the office of a "teacher". These were women of high standing in the Church, and yet they dared not to speak to this young teacher in a public forum.**

<u>Titus 2:3-8</u>

3 Likewise, teach the older women to be reverent in the way they live, not to be slanderers or addicted to much wine, but to teach what is good.

4 Then **they can train the younger women** to love their husbands and children,

5 to be self-controlled and pure, to be busy at home, to be kind, **and to be subject to their husbands, so that no one will malign the word of God.**

6 Similarly, encourage the young men to be self-controlled.

7 In everything set them an example by doing what is good. In your teaching show integrity, seriousness

8 and soundness of speech that cannot be condemned, **so that those who oppose you may be ashamed because they have nothing bad to say about us.** NIV

<u>2 Tim 3:14-16</u>

14 But as for you, continue in what you have learned and have become convinced of, because you know those from whom you learned it,

15 **and how from infancy you have known the holy Scriptures,** which are able to make you wise for salvation through faith in Christ Jesus.

❖ **This verse is sometimes used to prove that women had been teaching men in the Church but it is clear that this verse simply attests to the fact that this young man was taught of elder women as he was growing up. It in no way supports the notion that women are called to teach men. It only supports the fact they [women] are called to teach children as well as other women.**

Danny McDowell

John 14:28-29

28 "You heard me say, 'I am going away and I am coming back to you.' If you loved me, you would be glad that I am going to the Father, **for the Father is greater than I.**

❖ This is the example of "submission" that the New Testament speaks of. It is the MAN who is suppose to submit to Christ as Christ submitted to the Father. Likewise, women are to submit to their husbands in that same way as Christ submitted to the Father. Women must not teach men in the same way that men cannot teach Christ, and Christ would never usurp the Father. It was SATAN who was the USURPER, and women who usurp are following after that one who was not content with his high calling as the CROWNING CHERUB.

Phil 2:6-11

6 Who, being in very nature God,

did not consider equality with God something to be grasped,

7 **but made himself nothing,**

**taking the very nature of a servant,**

**being made in human likeness.**

8 **And being found in appearance as a man,**

**he humbled himself**

**and became obedient to death-**

**even death on a cross!**

9 Therefore God exalted him to the highest place

and gave him the name that is above every name,

10 that at the name of Jesus every knee should bow,

in heaven and on earth and under the earth,

11 and every tongue confess that Jesus Christ is Lord,

to the glory of God the Father.

❖ There is a certain **EXALTATION** to women who receive their earthly calling in grace and humility----just as Jesus humbled himself to the will of the Father, so also will women be rewarded for subjecting their own will to that of the Father.

1 Cor 15:28

*28 When he has done this, then the Son himself will be made subject to him who put everything under him, **so that God may be all in all.***

❖ This is the high calling of all of us-----to do the will of the Father. The New Testament is absolutely clear. So what is the problem? Why such turmoil over this issue of "authority in the Church"?. It actually boils down to a five letter word-----FLESH. "The heart is desperately wicked above all things---and who can know it". The heart of man simply cannot agree with the heart of God. The heart of man is inherently rebellious. It wants no part in those things which are contrary to its own will, whether that person is male or female. The heart cannot even distinguish good from evil in all matters. How many times have we had to take time to THINK----"is this right or would it be wrong?" We are all the same. It is only submission to the supernatural power of the Holy Spirit that can change that rebellion into willful submission----and beyond that, "joyful submission". That part of the discussion is not gender specific. It's you and it's me, male and female.

The fact is, we are trying to address the question that affects WOMEN in the Church----and "THAT" can become a **LAND MINE.**

The only way to address this topic is "openly" and straight forward. The effort at "Tact" and finesse seem condescending to many women, and so great drops of sweat burst forth on the brow of that man who would challenge a woman on her insistence that she is called to be a TEACHER of all. "After all" says she, "I know that I know that the Lord has called me to pastor and teach in this Church, and no one can tell me otherwise". She is quite correct in her statement-----"no one can tell her otherwise"----not God----and certainly not man. "But I have the anointing" she may say. That's wonderful---- now use that anointing in faithful service to your spiritual HUSBAND----which is Christ! When all is said and done, it is the will of God that we are talking about here.

What is the problem? What is so terrible about being limited to a mere SEVENTY PERCENT of the Church world? It is estimated that the great majority of Church attending Christians today are women. It is estimated that WOMEN and CHILDREN occupy 70% of that attendance. What is it in the nature of a woman that causes her to be so upset at the notion that she can minister to literally hundreds of millions of people without fear that she may be displeasing to the Lord in her ministry, and yet she cannot have authority over men-----the remaining thirty percent? What is the root of this attitude? The rebellion began in the Garden. It started with EVE.

It all began before the earth was ever created. It began in the mind of God. No Christian can deny this. God created man FIRST. Then he created woman from the rib of man. As the appointed HEAD over woman, Adam was held responsible for what Eve had done----because he was the HEAD over her. It has been the appointment of man to show leadership throughout the ages. It's truly NOT the motives of a "chauvinistic" God, to create man SUPERIOR to WOMAN. It's simply the sovereign will of a perfect creator. As a man in this world, I have not been appointed to rub my authority into the face of my wife. I am to view her as my EQUAL in terms of our mutual humanity. I am suppose to listen and learn from her as she listens and learns from me. This is the sign of a healthy Christian relationship. When it comes to the assembly of God's elect----a more defined role is Biblically shaped for both man and woman. A woman is not to preach to, or teach men. She is never authorized to usurp authority over a man at any time-----in the Church. This is the manifest will of a perfect God.

CHAPTER XII

Religious GARB

The wearing of Ceremonial religious robes and special clothing does in no way commend you to God nor disqualify you as a servant of God, for God looks upon the heart. So what is the real PURPOSE of "religious garb"? There can only be one answer. It is for "recognition" and can only be for that purpose. Since God is not impressed with what we wear over our skin, but rather, that which is beneath the skin. It is therefore a reasonable conclusion that robes, gowns, clerical collars, caps, miters and every such adornment is worn for the specific purpose of setting one apart from another. It is a vehicle of HIGHER RECOGNITION and NEVER the adornment of a servant. It is purely a matter of the flesh and it's appetite for recognition. As Christians, it is not the clothing we wear, nor the religious jewelry we express ourselves with, nor the bumper stickers we display, but rather----the "walk that we walk". We are epistles, known and read of men. I dare say, there was never an apostle of the New Testament that showed his piety in any other way than in the transparency of his life in Jesus Christ. Some may say----"I just believe that we ought to sport the very best we have in respect to our savior". Just try to challenge that fleshly excuse and you will soon meet the flesh face to face.

I wouldn't waste my time trying to convince anyone otherwise. It should be spiritually inherent in the Christian psyche------- The TEMPLE OF GOD is adorned from the inside outward into a modest attire, never using any accessory that would identify us as anyone different than anyone else. Oh the human pride in adorning one's self with those things that set us apart. You are no better for wearing religious garb, nor terribly worse----just simply FLESHLY!

I've spoken much about the "tribulation of the saints". It is clear to me that in our journey through those wretched days, there will be no place for "religious recognition"-------your life may depend on discretion and wisdom, for the Church shall be certainly----- an UNDERGROUND entity.

TRADITION---the POLLUTANT OF TRUTH

Matt 15:3-8

*3 Jesus replied, "And **why do you break the command of God for the sake of your tradition?***

4 For God said, 'Honor your father and mother' and 'Anyone who curses his father or mother must be put to death.'

5 But you say that if a man says to his father or mother, 'Whatever help you might otherwise have received from me is a gift devoted to God,'

*6 he is not to 'honor his father' with it. **Thus you nullify the word of God for the sake of your tradition.***

7 You hypocrites! Isaiah was right when he prophesied about you:

Mark 7:9-13

*9 And he said to them: "**You have a fine way of setting aside the commands of God in order to observe your own traditions!***

10 For Moses said, 'Honor your father and your mother,' and, 'Anyone who curses his father or mother must be put to death.'

*11 But you say that if a man says to his father or mother: '**Whatever help you might otherwise have received from me is Corban' (that is, a gift devoted to God),***

12 then you no longer let him do anything for his father or mother.

*13 **Thus you nullify the word of God by your tradition** that you have handed down. And you do many*

<u>2 Thess 3:6</u>

*6 In the name of the Lord Jesus Christ, we command you, brothers, to keep away from every brother who is idle and does not live **according to the teaching you received from us.***

<u>1 Peter 1:18-21</u>

*18 For you know that it was not with perishable things such as silver or gold that **you were redeemed from the empty way of life handed down to you from your forefathers,***

19 but with the precious blood of Christ, a lamb without blemish or defect.

20 He was chosen before the creation of the world, but was revealed in these last times for your sake.

*21 Through him you believe in God, who raised him from the dead and glorified him, **and so your faith and hope are in God.***

Tradition kills the spirit. It shoves the moving of the Spirit of God to the back of the bus. All kinds of traditions----religious tradition, cultural tradition, family tradition, social tradition, racial tradition, ethnic tradition, national tradition-----are mostly contrary to the CULTURE OF THE KINGDOM OF GOD. The sooner we can dispense with it, the better, for Jesus said "my Kingdom is NOT OF THIS WORLD".

CHAPTER XIII

Watchman-----COME DOWN OFF THAT WALL

The "watchman ministry" is different from most other ministries. Most people don't want to hear the sound of a fire truck headed toward their own home. You've experienced this I'm sure. You're out in your car and you pull over for the Fire Truck. The siren is wailing. Then you watch as it turns down your street. Quickly you step on the throttle to follow after. The first thing that has crossed your mind is that frightful question-----"could it be MY HOUSE"? You breathe a sigh of relief as you see the Fire Truck turn off your street and head away from your home. Everyone agrees that Firemen and Fire Trucks are a wonderful thing-----"but not at MY HOUSE". So it is with the "WATCHMAN MINISTRY". Nobody wants the watchman to turn down their street. The sight and sound of a Fire Truck is unpleasant. It means that "destruction" is at hand. No one waves or cheers as a Fire Truck goes by. All you think is, "I sure hope no one is hurt"

The "Watchman" is similar in that way. The sight and sound of him is not pleasant. He is not one to speak in low tones. Often his voice is like a siren and all you want to do is put your fingers in your ears, drop your head and close your eyes. The Watchman is not really WANTED in the Church, but like the Fireman, he is needed---especially in these days when the Church is so deeply corrupted. A Watchman is never one who "calls himself" into that ministry because the ministry itself is so unpleasant. Unlike the Fireman, the Watchman experiences curses and insults, even threats of physical harm as when a friend of mine was forced to hire body guards to accompany him as he preached in Kampala Uganda.

The Watchman loves and hates his calling at the same time. He loves the FIRE that rages in his bones as he preaches, teaches, or writes. He loves that because he knows that it is the Spirit of the Lord. Then come the harsh criticisms. Then comes the rejection. Then comes the personal confusion and doubt about one's own self-----worst of all, then comes the doubt about one's "calling" as a Watchman. In a short time, the Watchman is encouraged by the Lord and the Holy fire returns. Like seasoned oak, the fire burns hot and steady until the next idiot attempts to obstruct that spiritual FIRE TRUCK that is headed to his very own house. Here are some verses regarding the Watchman Ministry.

Ezek 33:1-17

33:1 Again the word of the LORD came unto me, saying,

2 Son of man, speak to the children of thy people, and say unto them, When I bring the sword upon a land, if the people of the land take a man of their coasts, and set him for their watchman:

3 If when he seeth the sword come upon the land, he blow the trumpet, and warn the people;

4 Then whosoever heareth the sound of the trumpet, and taketh not warning; if the sword come, and take him away, his blood shall be upon his own head.

5 He heard the sound of the trumpet, and took not warning; his blood shall be upon him. But he that taketh warning shall deliver his soul.

6 But if the watchman see the sword come, and blow not the trumpet, and the people be not warned; if the sword come, and take any person from among them, he is taken away in his iniquity; **but his blood will I require at the watchman's hand.**

7 So thou, O son of man, I have set thee a watchman unto the house of Israel; therefore thou shalt hear the word at my mouth, and warn them from me.

8 When I say unto the wicked, O wicked man, thou shalt surely die; if thou dost not speak to warn the wicked from his way, that wicked man shall die in his iniquity; but his blood will I require at thine hand.

9 Nevertheless, if thou warn the wicked of his way to turn from it; if he do not turn from his way, he shall die in his iniquity; but thou hast delivered thy soul.

10 Therefore, O thou son of man, speak unto the house of Israel; Thus ye speak, saying, If our transgressions and our sins be upon us, and we pine away in them, how should we then live?

11 Say unto them, As I live, saith the Lord GOD, I have no pleasure in the death of the wicked; but that the wicked turn from his way and live: turn ye, turn ye from your evil ways; for why will ye die, O house of Israel?

12 Therefore, thou son of man, say unto the children of thy people, The righteousness of the righteous shall not deliver him in the day of his transgression: as for the wickedness of the wicked, he shall not fall thereby in the day that he turneth from his wickedness; neither shall the righteous be able to live for his righteousness in the day that he sinneth.

13 When I shall say to the righteous, that he shall surely live; if he trust to his own righteousness, and commit iniquity, all his righteousnesses shall not be remembered; but for his iniquity that he hath committed, he shall die for it.

14 Again, when I say unto the wicked, Thou shalt surely die; if he turn from his sin, and do that which is lawful and right;

15 If the wicked restore the pledge, give again that he had robbed, walk in the statutes of life, without committing iniquity; he shall surely live, he shall not die.

16 None of his sins that he hath committed shall be mentioned unto him: he hath done that which is lawful and right; he shall surely live.

17 Yet the children of thy people say, The way of the Lord is not equal: **but as for them, their way is not equal.**

You who cause the watchman to stumble at his duty-----put your hand to your mouth for if that man's calling is from GOD-----you defy the Lord!

CLOSING

My earnest desire in closing is to encourage God's people to take responsibility for their Faith. So many have walked the path that I have walked for over twenty five years. I followed like a dumb sheep. If the Pastor said "this"----then those words were tantamount to the Gospel. If he said "that"----the same. The books I read were purchased from the local Christian book stores. Those same stores were pressured by organizations and denominations to stock ONLY books that measured up to their doctrinal parameters. There was a WILDERNESS to traverse. No one to teach me sound doctrine, no one to lead, no mentor to fall back on. It was lonely. If I lifted my voice, I was viewed as a KOOK. When I met a neighbor at the local grocery store, he/she would find a way to duck around to the next isle to avoid me. People would roll their eyes as they passed by. They whispered to one another as they walked away "he teaches false doctrine". I was hurt. I was lonely-----and then came the computer. Then I discovered that I was not alone. I found Roy Reinholdt, Richard Perry, Dave Mac Pherson, and dozens more. I began to meet people that had the same experience as myself. Then I discovered so many others who had walked a similar path. There was a vast pool of information on the internet. I sucked up the information like a dry sponge. Over a few years of time, I discovered that there was an enormous number of Watchman Ministries all over the world. Kizito Michael George and Kato Mivule in Uganda, Arvin Goney in India. I opened a "Watchman" website. Thousands and thousands of people read the site. From every continent on earth except Antarctica.

I discovered there are hundreds of thousands of us, perhaps millions who are tired of the Apostasy of the modern Church, people who are HOMESICK----HOMESICK for the New Testament and the sure continuity of the Word of God. If someone reads this book and is encouraged to GO BACK----GO BACK to the New Testament Faith, then this work will have been worth it all. I have taught Bible students here in the United States, and in Uganda East Africa. They are famished for sound doctrine for they are constantly under pressure from False Teaching and Heresy. American Heretics travel the world looking for one proselyte to drag into hell with them. The mighty words of Paul ring so true-----"our gathering SHALL NOT COME until there is that great APOSTASIA"----falling away.

Danny McDowell

Jer 2:13

13 "My people have committed two sins:

They have forsaken me,

the spring of living water,

and have dug their own cisterns,

broken cisterns that cannot hold water. NIV

Contact:
www.againstallheresy@gmail.com

John Burcham on Danny McDowell

Danny's style is, how can I put it, Eccentric without flamboyance. There really is no middle ground with Danny. You either agree with what he says about the Bible, or you will find yourself rationalizing your own belief system and the way you were taught. I have discovered that most people can't fight the logic of his arguments, but rather, they rely on teachers that they know personally and have grown up with. When presented with facts and evidence, the coping mechanism kicks in. They say "I know what you are saying seems to be true and I know what the Bible says BUT, you don't know my Pastor like I do. He is a great man. He would NEVER mislead me in any way". I have seen firsthand this message being presented and then rejected outright because no profit could be made on this style of teaching. This guy's system of teaching is too ancient, in fact it goes all the way back to the first century.

John Burcham

Missionary, Producer, Director, Video Choreography, Cameraman, Film Consultant.

COVER DESIGN : "APOSTASIA, a corrupt Church for a corrupt age".

Film Credits:

Breath Deniability
Stones of Fire
Junkyard Theology
The Gathering----a YouTube video
American Heretics in Uganda-----a YouTube video

contact: colcrusher@triad.rr.com